Cake Decorating Ornaments

by
NORMA DUNN

Cake Decorating Ornaments

Souvenir Press

Contents

First published in Australia
by Murray Book Distributors Pty. Limited.
Reprinted by Gregory's Publishing Company.

First published 1979
Reprinted 1981
Reprinted 1982
Reprinted 1983

Copyright © 1979 Norma Dunn

First British Edition
published 1983 by Souvenir Press Ltd.,
43 Great Russell Street, London WC1B 3PA

ISBN 0 285 62580 2

Designed by Jill Day
Typeset by Auckland Typographical Services
Printed by Toppan Printing Co.

PHOTOGRAPHY: Peter Bateman, Sydney.

Dedication
To my dear John, Ronald, Paul and Coral
Norma Dunn, 1978

Many books have been written on cake decorating, but over the years this art has grown to such an extent that it is impossible to provide a book of instruction which deals with all phases of cake decorating under the one cover. I feel there is a great demand for a cake decorating book to deal with one aspect of the art, and deal with it in detail, so that there will be not only a complete book of reference for that particular subject, but it will be a book of learning.

With that in mind I have written Cake Decorating Ornaments, which gives a wide variety of ornaments to make for cakes for every occasion; and also detailed instructions, patterns and how to use the result. Nothing has been left to guesswork, and I have designed ornaments for originality, appearance, daintiness and appeal. I consider that the cake decorator, with the instructions given, will have no difficulty in making them.

At the back of the book is a chapter on decorated cakes for many occasions, which I think will be found to be very helpful.

Writing this book has given me great satisfaction, because I feel that it will be appreciated by cake decorators, who are always looking for new ideas.

I know decorators will experience a wonderful sense of achievement after making their own ornaments, and that this book will give them many years of pleasure.

Two-tier Round Wedding Cake. Instructions, see page 172

Frangipani and large embroidered bell make a beautiful ornament for a wedding cake —
instructions page 76.

Roses and Fuchsias. Instructions, see page 174

11

1

Requirements for Moulding

REQUIREMENTS FOR MOULDING

1. Select a laminex-covered board about 30½ x 25 cm (12 x 8 inches) for rolling out and cutting.

2. A length of dowel about 28 cm long and 2 cm in diameter (11 inches long and ¾ inch in diameter) for rolling out a large amount of modelling paste. Sand well with fine sandpaper for a smooth surface.

3. A meat skewer for rolling out small pieces of modelling paste. Cut off the point, smooth with fine sandpaper and it is ready for use.

4. A small covered bowl of cornflour for dusting modelling board and rolling pin.

5. A pair of scissors for cutting out patterns.

6. A pair of very small scissors, necessary when cutting out small patterns such as animal motifs or similar.

7. A long-bladed knife to cut a long straight edge in one movement, such as a card or similar.

8. A scalpel. Essential when cutting out small patterns in modelling paste.

9. Tweezers to arrange flowers in ornaments.

10. A metric ruler.

11. Tracing paper.

12. A sharp-pointed pencil for tracing patterns.

13. Soft cardboard which may be bought at a newsagents, to cut patterns.

14. Modelling stick. This is used mainly when moulding flowers, but has been mentioned and used several times in this book to make some ornaments. It is made from an inexpensive paint brush. Buy size 00, cut off the handle, sand one end to a point and round the other to a smooth finish.

15. Paint brushes for painting completed ornaments. Buy good quality sable hair brushes – a No. 3 and No. 5 for general painting and a No. 00 for fine work.

16. Food colors. Start with basic colors, blue, green, burgundy, red, yellow, violet and brown. If you require black or white, use water color paint.

17. Painting tray. Use a tray with about 10 sections for mixing colors. Although the liquid will dry, the color may be used again with a damp brush.

18. Wire. Used for wiring flowers in some ornaments. I use a heavy gauge wire

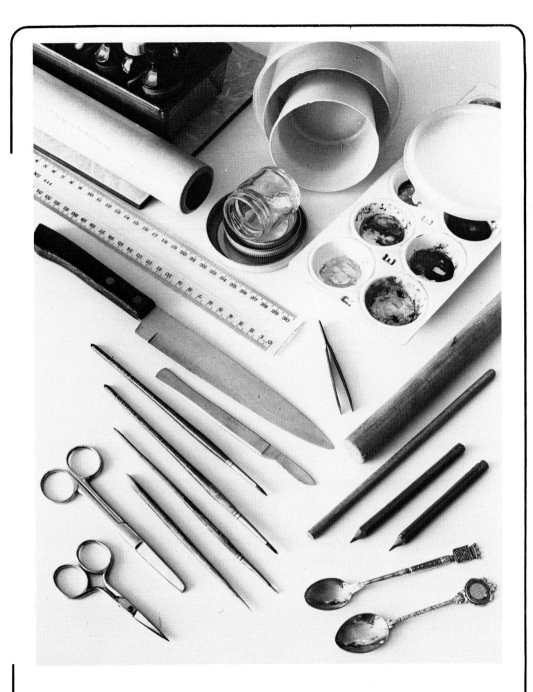

.0148 in Eureka resistance wire for flowers such as roses, daffodils, azaleas or similar, and .010 in Eureka resistance wire for all small flowers such as snowdrops, hyacinths or similar. A good general rule to follow is to use a wire as fine as possible, strong enough to support the flower and still give a dainty appearance. You can buy wire from a shop selling cake-decorating supplies, or approach a wire-manufacturing firm and buy a reel direct. When using wire, keep a small bowl of water on hand for dipping tip of wire to attach flowers.

2
Hints for the Decorator

HINTS FOR THE DECORATOR

Before starting to mould any ornaments, please read and observe the following points which you will find very helpful.

1. Before beginning, collect everything you will require for moulding.

2. Wear an apron.

3. Prepare a bowl of freshly sieved icing sugar, which will be required when working-up modelling paste.

4. A damp cloth to wipe your hands, and a hand towel.

5. To ensure paste does not stick, keep modelling board and rolling pin lightly dusted with cornflour. There is no need to use a lot of cornflour, it only dries the paste. Keep moving paste around on board when cutting out.

6. To obtain the correct consistency for making ornaments, it is necessary to work additional icing sugar into the modelling paste as you use it. Should the paste stick after dusting board and rolling pin with cornflour, it is a sign paste is too soft. Re-knead, and add more icing sugar. If paste cracks, it is too dry – add a little more soft paste. Paste should roll out smoothly. If there are signs of cracking beforehand, rolling out will not remove them and cracks will show up on the finished article.

7. Whether rolling out a small or large amount of paste, always roll into a smooth ball onto the palm of your hand before rolling out.

8. The top of a souvenir spoon handle pressed evenly and firmly around the edge of a plaque or similar gives an attractive finish.

9. To avoid breakages, transfer finished article or parts onto another board to set.

10. After ornaments are completed, unless required immediately, pack away carefully and keep in a dry place. Some silica gel crystals are good for this purpose, although not a necessity. Obtainable from a chemist, they are a deep blue/violet when dry and change to pink after absorbing moisture. To dry, spread on a tray and place in a very slow oven about 120 deg. C (250 deg. F) until they return to blue. Do not have oven too hot or you will burn them.

11. Never leave ornaments on a table to dry in wet weather. The moisture from the air will be absorbed. Place in a cupboard.

12. Modelling paste must be thoroughly dried before painting, otherwise color could run. Leave several days if possible.

13. To avoid color running when painting, let one color dry before painting another color next to it.

14. If you make a mistake when painting, remove color carefully with a damp brush, leave to dry, then repaint. It is a good idea when moulding to roll out a spare piece of paste to test colors.

15. The soft cardboard in greeting cards is excellent for cutting patterns. A card itself is an accurate pattern if you wish to make a card from modelling paste.

16. When cutting out a pattern where it is necessary for both sides to be exactly the same, such as a vase, christening mug or similar, draw a pattern and fold in half. Cut through the centre. Place half the pattern on the fold of the paper and cut out. Open out and carefully cut another pattern, so that the crease does not mark the paste.

17. All patterns must be cut cleanly around the edge with scissors to ensure a smooth edge when cutting out in modelling paste.

18. To enable you to find patterns quickly, place each pattern in a small plastic bag. It will not only protect them, they will be easily seen and quickly found when required.

19. Use the top of screw-top jars, basins and soft plastic containers – in fact anything suitable for cutting out round plaques or similar. It is a lot easier and more accurate than cutting a pattern.

3 Moulded Ornaments

1. Small glass jar used as a mould to make flower pot (right). Instructions page 88. 2. Beer stein pattern instructions page 88. Plaque, how to wire tulle and ribbon for posy of spring flowers or similar — instructions opposite.

A LIFT-OFF POSY OF SPRING FLOWERS

See page: 30
Daffodils, jonquils, Cecil Brunner roses, snowdrops, violets and hyacinths make a lovely lift-off posy of spring flowers suitable for an anniversary, birthday or Mother's Day cake.
Have all flowers made and painted to arrange immediately into base.

Flowers required: 3 daffodils (yellow with orange centre)
3 sprays jonquils (each spray containing 1 flower with yellow centre, white outside petals, 1 partly-opened flower and 2 buds)
3 apricot roses   6 mauve hyacinths
12 snowdrops   3 maidenhair fern
5 violets

Base:
Roll out modelling paste with dowel so that centre is about 1 cm (3/8 inch) thick tapering to edge, and cut a circle about 8½ cm (3¼ inches). Mark around edge with top of handle of a souvenir spoon to give an attractive finish as shown.

To assemble:
1. Pleat a piece of tulle with fingers about 20 x 10 cm (8 x 4 inches) and twist a short length of wire around centre. Loop ribbon securing at base with a twist of wire.

2. Place tulle and ribbon into centre and arrange flowers. Leave flat until completely set.

ENGAGEMENT PLAQUE

Ornament: See page 30
A delightful plaque suitable for a young couple's engagement cake has been made using a tracing of a picture from an engagement wrapping paper. Always choose a design with clear and simple lines.

To make plaque:
1. Roll out modelling paste (do not color) with dowel as finely as practicable, and cut a circle about 10 cm (4 inches) or size to suit chosen motif.

2. Mark around edge to give an attractive finish with the top of handle of a souvenir spoon.

3. Trace pattern carefully, marking in all details.

4. Transfer tracing on to plaque. Refer instructions Santa Claus page 61

5. Carefully paint with food colors. To avoid color running, do not paint one color next to another until it is dry.

6. Designs such as this will be greatly improved, if you finally outline motifs with a fine brush and brown food coloring.

23

SHOWER UMBRELLA

Decorated cake – Shower for Jan: See page 177

A cake featuring an umbrella filled with flowers is a delightful way to celebrate the happy occasion.

To make umbrella: Mould in color.
1. Cut pattern.

2. Roll out modelling paste with dowel as finely as practicable, place pattern in position, and carefully cut out with scalpel. Mark as shown with scalpel and place over the side of a bowl to curve. Leave until set.

3. Using a No. 00 tube and royal icing, embroider and add a tiny scalloped edge around top.

To make handle:
1. Handle measures about 16 cm (6¼ inches). Bind several thicknesses of flower wire or a pipe cleaner with narrow satin ribbon. Bend to shape handle.

2. Gather a small length of tulle 2.5 cm deep (1 inch) as shown, securing with needle and cotton.

To assemble:
1. Position umbrella on cake.

2. Place a small length of wire through the back of a knot ribbon bow and bend to form a U shape. Place over handle and insert into cake to hold in position.

3. Arrange flowers.

Pattern

25

Pattern

26

CUP AND SAUCER

Decorated cake: See page 177
A cup and saucer filled with flowers is something different and suitable for a shower tea or birthday cake.

To make cup and saucer:
1. Cut a pattern. Note – adjust saucer pattern when cutting out to fit snugly around cup.

2. Cup: Roll out modelling paste with dowel as finely as practicable, place pattern in position, and cut out with a scalpel. Place a little cotton wool beneath top edge, round sides and base with fingers making sure they are touching surface. Leave to dry.

3. Saucer: Roll out paste as above and cut out saucer. Leave flat to dry.

4. Handle: Roll a small ball of paste beneath finger tips to a pencil shape, curve quickly to form handle and cut either end with scalpel to fit cup.

5. With a No. 00 tube and royal icing, embroider cup and saucer with a tiny scallop as shown. When dry, tip gold. Paint a little food coloring around the edge of saucer in a deeper shade to match cup and saucer to accentuate shape.

HEARTS AND FLOWERS

Hearts combine with fuchsias and jasmine to make a very attractive arrangement for an engagement cake.

To make hearts: Measurements across top also through the centre 3 cm (1¼ inches)

Note – make hearts large enough to take name.

1. Cut a pattern. To cut an accurate pattern, see Hints for the Decorator No. 16.

2. Roll out modelling paste with dowel about 3 mm (⅛ inch) thick, place pattern in position and cut out with scalpel. Smooth around top edge with finger.

3. Bend a length of flower wire about 6 cm (2¼ inches) into a U shape and insert immediately in back as shown and leave to dry.

4. With a No. 00 tube and royal icing, pipe a tiny scallop around edge of hearts, pipe names and tip in silver when dry.

Flowers required: 3 pink double fuchsias
2 mauve double fuchsias
12 jasmine flowers and 12 buds
2 maidenhair fern

5. Arrange flowers, position hearts.

Top: Orchids and lily-of-the-valley, a perfect combination for a silver wedding anniversary cake — instructions page 78.
Bottom: A lovely floral arrangement with hearts for an engagement cake — instructions above.

Top: Spring flowers make an ideal ornament for a birthday cake — instructions see page 23.
Above: Instructions for making this delightful plaque see page 23.

An open umbrella filled with roses makes a lovely ornament for a special occasion cake — instructions see page 99.

LIFT-OFF POSY OF FULL BLOWN ROSES

Popular full blown roses make a lift-off posy for a birthday cake.
Flowers required: 2 full blown roses
                     about 2 doz. small flowers
                     3 rose leaves

Have flowers made and painted to arrange immediately into plaque. Small flowers illustrated are not a true flower, but are quickly and easily made, and are quite attractive. To make flower, roll a tiny piece of firm modelling paste into a cone. Using scalpel, cut a cross into the top like a hot cross bun. Resting on forefinger, insert pointed end of modelling stick into the centre, and with a roll and press motion, shape each section to form four petals. Insert length of fine hooked wire down through the centre, firming at base with fingers. Leave to set. Paint any color desired. For variation, leave white and add a touch of yellow in the centre or add a colored stamen.

Plaque:
Roll out modelling paste with dowel, about 4 mm ($^3/_{16}$ inch) thick tapering to the edge, and cut a circle about 8½ cm (3¼ inches).

To assemble:
1. Insert tulle and looped ribbon towards back of base (to make, see posy of spring flowers) page 23

2. Attach roses with royal icing.

3. Arrange small flowers and leaves. Leave flat to dry.

RING CASE

Floral decoration: See page 51

An attractive ring case can be made from a plastic one which may be bought from a shop selling cake-decorating supplies.

Medium roses and jasmine have been arranged with a ring case to make a lovely ornament suitable for a single-tier wedding cake, the top tier of a two or three-tier wedding cake or with an engagement ring, for an engagement cake.

Flowers required: 3 medium roses which have been wired
                   2 doz. jasmine flowers
                   2 doz. jasmine buds
                   4 rose leaves

Note – in this arrangement, ring case has been set on a small cushion of modelling paste to elevate it.

To make ring case:

1. Separate ring case as shown.

2. Roll out firm modelling paste (in color if preferred) as finely as practicable, and place over the outside of the well cornfloured plastic ring case. Carefully press over the complete surface firmly with fingers, making sure not to miss any spot or the design will not come out.

3. Remove, place on modelling board and carefully cut around edge with scalpel.

4. Cornflour the inside of the ring case and place inside. Tip out to make sure it is not sticking, replace, and leave to set. Make the other half the same way. When dry, it is ready to assemble.

To assemble:

1. Take sufficient modelling paste to fill the base to give a slightly rounded appearance. Lightly moisten base with a little water so it will stick, place cushion of paste (which must be smooth and free of any cracks) into base, and with fingers, taper to the edge.

2. Press the tip of a souvenir spoon handle around the edge. It will give not only an attractive finish, but will also help to firm the edge.

3. Press ring into centre. If desired, two rings may be used. Lie flat, one resting on the other and secure with a little royal icing.

4. Place lid carefully into position and secure with royal icing. Use some support until lid sets – a little cotton wool will do.

5. Attach a small ribbon bow with royal icing where the lid is joined at the back.

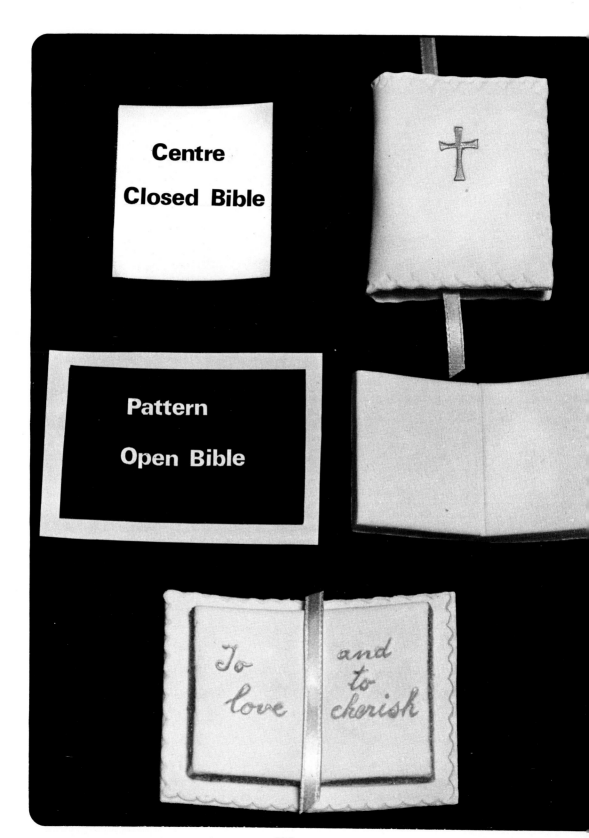

Centre

Closed Bible

Pattern

Open Bible

CLOSED BIBLE AND OPEN BIBLE

Full blown roses and jasmine have been arranged with a slim white candle and open Bible to make a lovely wedding ornament. A closed Bible could be substituted.

Flowers required: 3 full blown roses (2 large and 1 smaller which have been wired to elevate the arrangement)
18 jasmine flowers and 15 buds
3 rose leaves

Instructions for making candle: See index under candles. Graduated candle measures 13 cm (5 inches). To position candle, cut a small circle out of cake covering just large enough to hold candle and about 1 cm deep (⅜ inch). Squeeze a little royal icing into hole, insert candle, support if necessary and leave to completely set before arranging flowers.

Arrange flowers, rest Bible against candle as shown, securing along base of Bible with a run of royal icing. See page 50

Method for making closed Bible:

1. Cut pattern: Centre 5 x 6.5 cm (2 x 2½ inches) and 1 cm (⅜ inch) thick
Cover about 12 x 7.5 cm (4¾ x 3 inches). This will give a clearance of 5 mm top and bottom (about ¼ inch) and along front of Bible and allow for cover to wrap around back.

2. Centre: Roll out firm modelling paste with dowel about 1 cm (⅜ inch) thick, place pattern in position, and cut out cleanly with a long bladed knife. Make a small slit top and bottom with scalpel to insert ribbon later. You will find it easier to add cover if you leave centre to set first.

3. Cover: Roll out modelling paste with dowel as finely as practicable, place pattern in position and cut out cleanly with a long-bladed knife. Using top of souvenir spoon handle, press around edge as shown, which becomes the outside of the cover.

4. Lightly moisten back and front of centre with water and wrap cover immediately around the centre. Place flat to dry and press a small cross, bought on a chain at a department store, into cover. Remove. Alternatively, pipe a cross with a No. 2 or 3 tube.

5. Tip sides of book and cross with either silver or gold when dry. Insert ribbon (2 pieces) and secure with a little royal icing.

Method for making open Bible:

1. Cut pattern: Centre 7.5 x 5 cm (3 x 2 inches) and about 7 mm (¼ inch) thick
Cover about 9 x 6.5 cm (3½ x 2½ inches)

2. Centre: Roll out firm modelling paste with dowel, place pattern in position and cut out cleanly with a long-bladed knife. Mark down the centre with a ruler.

3. Cover: Roll out modelling paste with dowel as finely as practicable and cut out as for centre. Lightly moisten back of centre with water, and attach cover making sure it is centred.

4. Using a No. 00 tube, pipe appropriate wording and scallop around cover of book.

5. Tip sides of book and writing in silver or gold and place ribbon down the centre, securing with a dot of royal icing.

WEDDING VASE

Pattern and vase of flowers: See opposite

Jasmine, lily-of-the-valley and hyacinths have been arranged to make a very attractive vase for a wedding cake, using a small tin dish as shown which may be bought in any large hardware store.

Method:
Top. Roll out modelling paste as finely as practicable, place in dish which has been cornfloured and trim around edge cleanly with a knife. Tip out to make sure it is not sticking, replace and leave to dry.

Base.
Roll out modelling paste and cut a circle 2½ cm (1 inch) and about 4 mm ($^3/_{16}$ inch) thick. Press the tip of a souvenir spoon around the edge as shown and leave to set. Attach to top with royal icing, making sure to set it in the centre.
To arrange flowers:
Brush inside of vase with a little water so icing will adhere, and add sufficient modelling paste so it is rounded in the centre and tapering to the edge. Wire flowers immediately into vase using tulle and loops of ribbon (see posy of spring flowers page 23) to soften the arrangement. It also helps to support the flowers and conceal the wire. Make sure you have sufficient flowers made as the paste sets quickly.

Flowers required: 4 sprays lily-of-the-valley
                     18 jasmine flowers and 12 buds
                     24 hyacinths and 12 buds

TULLE CHRISTENING FROCK AND BONNET

Frock and bonnet may be used on a large cake with a small spray of suitable flowers such as Cecil Brunner roses and snowdrops arranged around top of frock and bonnet.
Bonnet alone or frock alone could be used in the same way on a small cake.

Method for christening frock:
Bodice pattern: Length from shoulder to waist 5 cm (2 inches)
                         Waist measurement 7 cm (2¾ inches)
                         Shoulder measurement 4 cm (1½ inches)
Place pattern on fold of material at shoulder, also on centre of bodice, so you are actually cutting through four thicknesses of tulle (one quarter of the bodice). After cutting, open out and fold at shoulders.

Skirt: Cut piece of tulle 40 cm (16 inches) long and 12 cm (4¾ inches) deep. Fold width in half, then in half again (four thicknesses). Now fold equally into three. Pin carefully through all thicknesses to hold firmly and cut a scallop. Open out and frock will have 12 scallops around the lower edge. Fold skirt so the join is at the centre back slightly lapping.

To assemble frock:
1. Using needle and cotton, gather top edge of skirt (two thicknesses) to fit waist of frock.

2. Lap bodice (two thicknesses) over top of skirt and hand stitch.

3. Place frock over a dark background so you can see to embroider. With a No. 00 tube and royal icing of a soft consistency so it will adhere to tulle, embroider back of frock in a simple design. Reverse and embroider front. Handle carefully, as pipe work is delicate. Repair if necessary when placing on cake. Conceal stitching at waist with embroidery.

4. Slip a pin behind two small ribbon bows, insert through frock to attach to cake. They may be removed when cutting the cake.

Method for making bonnet:
1. Cut a circle 2½ cm (1 inch) in diameter.

2. Cut a piece of tulle about 12 cm long x 5 cm deep (4½ x 2 inches). Fold as for skirt, cutting into six tiny scallops.

3. Gather straight edge to fit about three quarters of the circle and stitch by hand.

4. Embroider as shown with a No. 00 tube and royal icing. Ribbon has been cut in half, looped, stitched, and bonnet attached to cake as for frock.

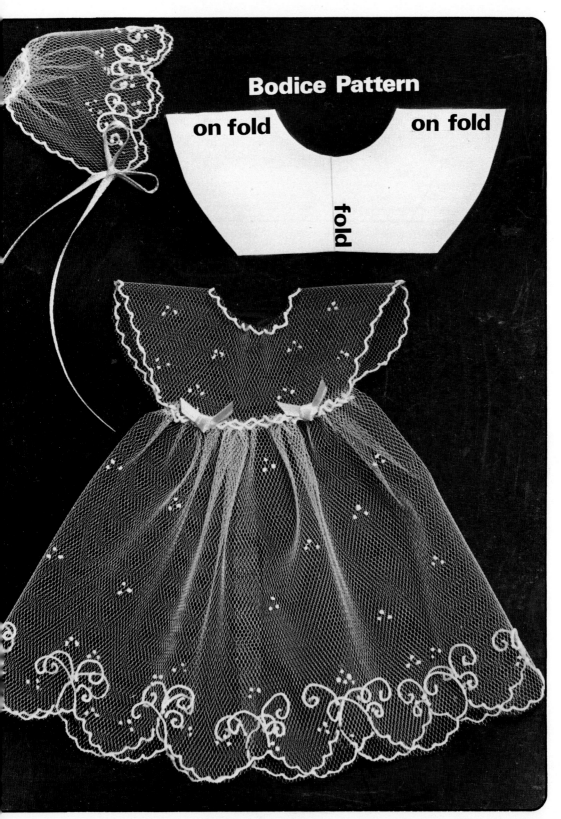

Bodice Pattern

on fold   on fold

fold

Pattern

CHRISTENING MUG

A christening mug, framed with sprays of dainty flowers or filled with tiny flowers, makes a lovely ornament for a christening cake.

To make christening mug framed with flowers:
1. Cut a pattern. Overall height about 6½ cm (2½ inches)
Width across centre and base 3½ cm (1⅜ inches)

2. Roll out modelling paste with dowel as finely as practicable, place pattern in position, and cut out with scalpel. Lie flat to dry.

3. Roll a small ball of paste back and forth beneath finger tips into a thin pencil shape. Cut a length sufficient to make handle, bend quickly to shape as shown. Leave to dry.

4. Embroider with a No. OO tube and royal icing.

5. When dry, paint silver.

6. Place on cake, attaching with royal icing and arrange flowers.
Flowers required: each spray 3 karume azaleas
4 ballerina fuchsias
5 snowdrops
2 maidenhair fern

To make christening mug filled with flowers:
Make in the same manner as described for christening mug framed with flowers. Use the same pattern, and when cutting out, cut along the lower edge at the top. Place a little cotton wool under the top edge to shape.
Flowers required: 10 snowdrops
12 moulded forget-me-nots
4 single stems maidenhair fern

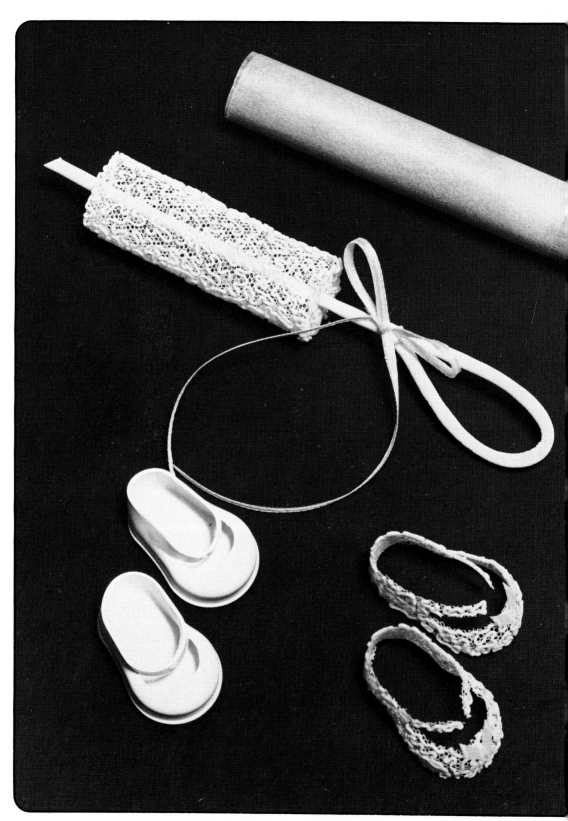

NET RATTLE AND
NET BOOTEES

A net rattle and net bootees make a dainty decoration for a christening cake. You could use them separately if you wish.

Net rattle:
1. Mould the handle. Roll out a small ball of modelling paste back and forth beneath finger tips into a long pencil shape about 22 cm (8¾ inches). Bend quickly to shape as shown and leave flat to dry.

2. Rattle: Cut a piece of cotton net about 7 cm long (2¾ inches) and wide enough to fit around dowel (used for rolling out) and lap slightly to join. Wrap a piece of waxed paper around dowel and secure with sticky tape.

3. Dip cotton net in stiffener (see recipe page 186), pat out surplus moisture on a towel, and place around dowel. Leave to dry. Remove.

4. With a No. 00 tube, embroider with cornelli work. Stand on end to dry.

5. Cut two ends for rattle You will find it easier to stiffen a small piece of cotton net when making 3, and leave flat to dry on waxed paper. Using end of dowel as a pattern, cut two small circles to fit rattle. Cut a tiny hole in each end to fit handle firmly.

6. Assemble rattle and embroider cornelli work over joins to hold ends in position. Support between two objects to dry.

7. Attach ribbon bow. Handle carefully.

Net bootees: Use a pair of plastic doll's shoes as a pattern.

1. Cut a pattern. A sole is not necessary. See moulded bootees. Page 55

2. Cut out in cotton net, allowing net to lap slightly where it joins at back.

3. Dip in net stiffener, pat lightly on towel to absorb any surplus moisture, and place on plastic shoes which have been greased lightly with a little butter. Leave to set.

4. Remove, easing around base with a needle.

5. Embroider with a No. 00 tube and royal icing and attach a ribbon bow.

BIB

A dainty bib featuring two little rabbits finely moulded and a spray of Cecil Brunner roses and forget-me-nots would make a lovely decoration for a christening cake. Pink and blue forget-me-nots and sprigs of grass have been painted directly on to the bib with food coloring.

To make bib:
1. Cut pattern, place into position on cake and outline carefully with a darning needle.

2. Bib may be made either in modelling paste or plastic icing. If you wish to keep bib, make it in modelling paste. Roll out icing with dowel, place pattern in position, and cut out with scalpel. Smooth around the edge with fingertips.

3. Brush over cake surface with a little water where bib has been outlined and position icing bib directly on to the outlined bib. Leave to set. Note – bib may be allowed to set and then placed on to cake if you wish to keep it.

4. Place rabbits on bib with royal icing. To make rabbits see page 108

5. Paint forget-me-nots and sprigs of grass.

6. Using a No. 00 tube, outline a tiny scallop and dot around edge of bib.

7. Arrange spray.

8. Attach lace.
Spray: 8 Cecil Brunner roses
        6 forget-me-nots
        2 maidenhair fern
        Loops pink ribbon. Width has been cut in half for a dainty appearance.

BON VOYAGE

Some Australian wildflowers arranged on a map of Australia would make an ideal ornament for a bon voyage cake.

To make map of Australia:
Use a plastic map (width 15 cm about 6 inches) which can be bought at a newsagent or trace a map from an atlas.

Method:
Roll out pale green modelling paste with dowel as finely as practicable, place pattern in position and cut out with scalpel. Leave flat to dry. If using a plastic map, press on to paste to obtain markings.
Flowers required: 1 waratah
                      2 sprays Christmas bells (each spray containing 4 or 5 flowers and 3 or 4 buds)
                      2 flannel flowers
                      2 sprays wattle
                      2 sprays each of brown boronia, pink boronia and Christmas bush (each spray containing 3 flowers)
All flowers must be painted and completely dry before attempting to arrange.

To assemble:
Mould some green modelling paste the same color as map into a banana shape sufficiently large to arrange the flowers, and attach to map with a little water. Arrange flowers into this with loops of red ribbon as shown. When arrangement is completed, paste should not be seen.

WELCOME HOME

Pattern of boomerang and motifs: See page 130

A kookaburra, koala and kangaroo with a boomerang on a map of Australia, makes a novel decoration for a welcome home cake.
To make map of Australia: See bon voyage above. Knead a little brown food coloring into paste.

Motifs and boomerang:
1. Cut patterns smaller to fit map.

2. Roll out a small ball of modelling paste finely with skewer, place pattern in position, and carefully cut out with scalpel one motif at a time as paste will set quickly.

3. When dry, paint with brown food coloring, marking in details in a deeper brown. Attach to map with royal icing. Paint branches for koala and kookaburra directly on to map.

4. Pipe welcome home on boomerang with a No. 00 tube and royal icing.

Bon Voyage

Welcome Home

A lovely floral arrangement with Bible and candle, ideal for a wedding cake — instructions see page 37.

CHRISTENING CARD

A christening card such as this is a lovely and unusual idea for a christening cake and may be made well in advance. If storing, place on a board to ensure it stays flat.

To make card:
Card measures about 17½ x 12½ cm (7 x 5 inches)
Insert measures about 11½ x 6½ cm (4½ x 2½ inches)

1. Roll out modelling paste in blue (or color of own choice) with dowel as finely as practicable. Use actual card as a pattern to ensure straight sides, and cut out with a long-bladed knife. Leave flat to dry.

2. Cut out insert in the same way (white).

3. Attach insert to card with a little royal icing, making sure it is centred.

4. Card must be completely set and dry before attempting to paint. Motifs are painted freehand on to card as shown. If you feel you are unable to do this, roll out modelling paste very finely with skewer, and cut out suitable motifs using a pattern. Leave to dry, paint and attach to card with royal icing.

5. Brush a little blue food coloring around the edges on insert, tapering to nothing in the centre. While still wet, sprinkle lightly with glitter.

6. With a No. 00 tube and royal icing, pipe wording and when dry, tip silver. Add blue ribbon bow.

MOULDED BOOTEES

Bootees can be easily made from modelling paste and are suitable for a christening cake.

1. Moulded bootees: These have been made over a pair of plastic doll's shoes. First cut a pattern. Roll out modelling paste with skewer finely, place pattern in position and cut out with scalpel. Place over plastic shoes which have been cornfloured on the outside, and join at the back with a touch of water. Leave to set. Remove. Cut out small straps, moisten each end with water and position as shown. Embroider with a No. 00 tube and add ribbon bow. Note – bootees have no sole.

2. Single bootee: Cut pattern. Roll out modelling paste with dowel as for 1 and cut out with scalpel. Place a little cotton wool under top edge as shown and leave to set. Embroider with cornelli work as shown, and place a ribbon and bow around bootee, attaching with royal icing. Place in position on cake and arrange flowers.

Flowers required: 12 apple blossom
                          7 forget-me-nots
                          2 maidenhair fern

Bootee may be also mounted on a plaque.

3. Hand-moulded bootees: Take two small balls of modelling paste the same size so both bootees will be the same size when completed. Leave one piece covered while you work the other. Have paste firm but soft enough to allow you time to make the bootee before it cracks.

You will find the rounded end of your modelling stick very helpful when shaping the bootee.

Pierce the centre and work to form the toe. Place index finger into the opening to complete shaping. Work around the bootee as shown, using the modelling stick and your fingers to form the sides and back.

Roll out paste very finely with skewer and cut two tiny straps. Bend to fit bootees, and when dry, attach at back with a run of royal icing. Embroider with a No. 00 tube and attach tiny bow. Small bow: Cut ribbon in half, then cut two small pieces so they are mitred at the join.

1. Bootees made in modelling paste using a pair of plastic doll's shoes. 2. Single bootee filled with apple blossom and forget-me-nots. 3. Hand moulded bootees.

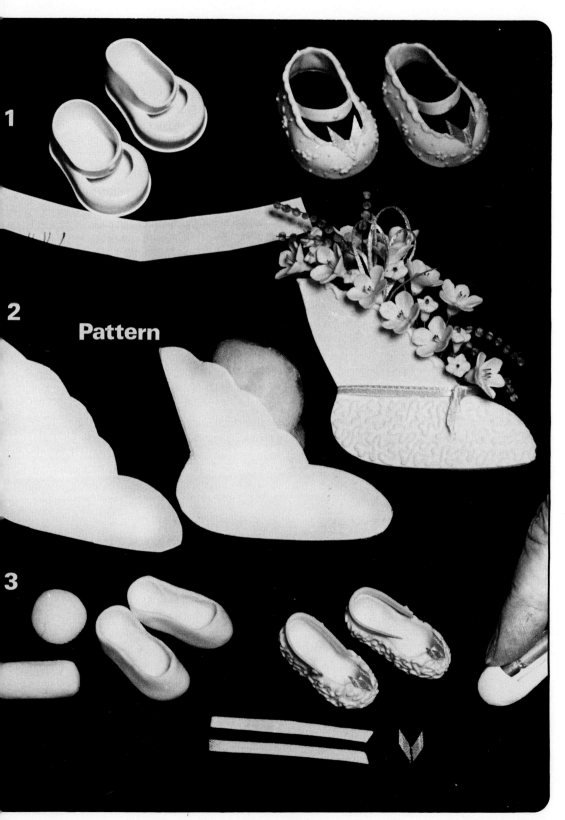

1

2

Pattern

3

55

CRIB

A dainty crib can be made from modelling paste into a lovely ornament for a christening cake.

To make crib:

1. Rockers: Roll out a small ball of paste beneath fingers to form a narrow pencil shape as shown, and cut two rockers 4 cm (1½ inches). Flatten each end with thumb and forefinger. Leave to dry.

2. Crib pattern measurements:
 2 sides each 6 cm x 13 mm (2⅜ x ½ inch)
 2 ends each 2½ cm x 13 mm (1 x ½ inch)
 base 6 x 2½ cm (2⅜ x 1 inch)
Roll out modelling paste with dowel as finely as practicable, place pattern in position, and cut out sides and ends using long-bladed knife (scalpel for curved ends). Cut out base slightly thicker. Leave to set and dry before assembling.

3. To assemble: Assemble on modelling board. Place base in position, run a little royal icing around all edges, and stand sides and ends in position. If necessary, support until set.

4. Attach rockers with royal icing. Leave until set.

5. Net support: 13 cm long (5 inches). Use several thicknesses of flower wire or a pipe cleaner. Bind with satin ribbon securing each end with needle and cotton. Bend at 10 cm (4 inches) and form a small circle as shown.

6. Net: Cut a piece of tulle 30½ cm long (12 inches) and about 9 cm (3½ inches) deep. Scallop with scissors around base (10 scallops) and two sides (3 scallops each side). Gather top edge with needle and cotton and draw to fit top of net support as shown. Stitch into place with needle and cotton.

7. Mattress: Using crib base pattern, roll out paste and cut a small mattress about 3 mm (⅛ inch) thick. Immediately place into crib. Cut a small pillow to fit and place in crib.

8. Insert net support through pillow and mattress, which should hold it firmly, and leave to dry.

9. Place doll in crib.

10. Crib cover:
 Measurements: 4½ cm (1¾ inches) wide and 4 cm (1½ inches) long.
 Cut 3 scallops each side as shown.
Roll out modelling paste very finely with skewer, place pattern in position, and cut out with scalpel. Immediately place crib cover over doll in crib and leave to set.

11. Carefully remove doll and crib cover and paint a forget-me-not and leaf design on pillow and crib cover. When dry, replace doll and cover.

12. With a No. 00 tube and royal icing, pipe a scallop around edge of crib cover and tiny scallops around net.

ANGELS

Follow these instructions to make an attractive decoration for a Christmas cake.

To make angels: Roll out paste in color of own choice.
1. Cut skirt pattern.

2. Roll out firm modelling paste (so that it will stand up when rolled) with dowel as finely as practicable, place pattern in position, and cut out sides with a long-bladed knife, and bottom edge with scalpel.

3. Roll to form skirt, and butt edges together at back, joining with a little water. Stand upright to dry.

4. Cut pattern for wings.

5. Roll out paste finely with skewer, place pattern in position, and cut out with scalpel.

6. Bend arms as shown, and leave flat to dry. Test over skirt first for correct position.

7. Head: Roll a little modelling paste into a smooth marble-sized ball, and insert tip of paint brush handle into ball (test on top of skirt for fit). Set aside to dry.

8. Place back on to paint brush handle and paint head. Leave to dry.

9. Halo: Roll a tiny piece of paste between fingers to form a thin pencil shape. Bend to form a tiny ring, joining with a dab of water.

To assemble:
1. Brush a little egg white around base of skirt, backs of wings and top of halo, and sprinkle with a little glitter.

2. Place wings over skirt.

3. Position head and halo with royal icing. Touch up arms with pink.

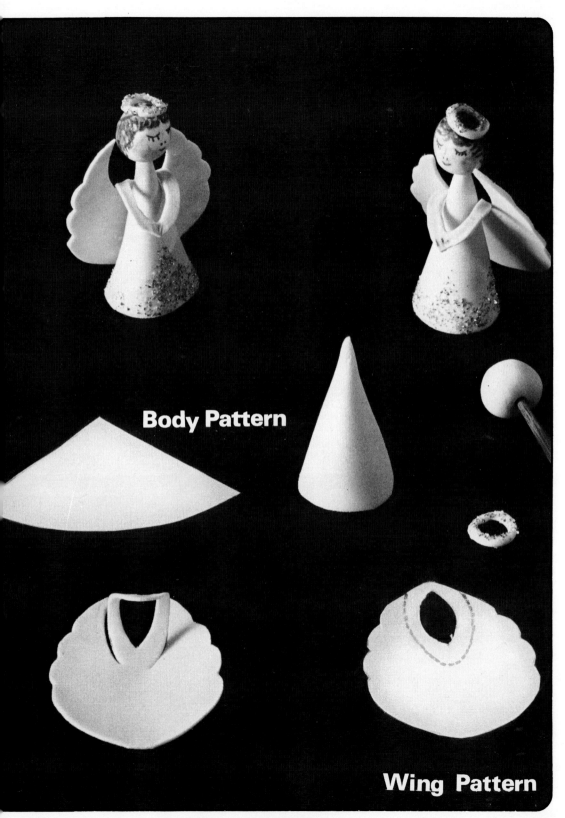

Body Pattern

Wing Pattern

Santa Tracing
and Pattern

Pattern traced on
to modeling past[e]

SANTA CLAUS

Jolly Santa with his frothy white beard and twinkling eyes will have special appeal as a Christmas cake decoration. It may be made well in advance and if you follow these instructions, you will find it quite simple to make. You will find a suitable Santa on a Christmas card.

1. Trace pattern, marking in all details.

2. Cut a pattern from tracing or cut out Santa from card and use as a pattern.

3. Roll out modelling paste with dowel as finely as practicable, place pattern in position, and cut out with scalpel.

4. Leave until paste has set sufficiently (test after three hours), place tracing on paste, and with sharp pencil, trace firmly on to modelling paste. Note – when you trace firmly with pencil, a guide line should be left on paste without the pencil sinking into paste. If it does, paste has not set sufficiently, so leave a little longer. If you leave it too long, paste will set hard and an imprint will not show. Remove tracing and mark guideline lightly with a pencil. You might find it easier to mark in pencil as you work.

5. Squeeze a little firm royal icing with a No. 3 tube to form whiskers and eyebrows. With a slightly damp brush, brush in the direction as shown to mark. Now work beard in the same way, brushing through with brush to obtain a realistic effect.

6. Squeeze royal icing around edge of cap and pom pom and rough up with brush. Leave to completely set and dry (a day or two if possible) before attempting to paint.

7. Paint with food colors, painting a small section at a time, and constantly referring to the original for shading.

CHRISTMAS ROSES, HOLLY AND CANDLES

A beautiful Christmas decoration has been made combining Christmas roses, holly and red candles set on a gold candlestick.

To make candlestick:
Legs:
1. Roll a small ball of modelling paste out finely with skewer, and cut three strips 4 x 1 cm (1½ x ⅜ inch). Very quickly curl one end around tip of modelling stick and place over a skewer or pencil as shown. Leave to set.

Top: (cut two) Only one top is set on legs, the other is positioned directly onto cake.
1. Roll out modelling paste with dowel as finely as practicable, and cut two circles about 5½ cm (2¼ inches) in diameter.

2. Flute around the edges by placing the tip of modelling stick at the back and pinch over the top with fingers. Keep moving it around and fluting with fingers until the circle is completed.

3. Place inside the lid of a screw-top jar measuring 5½ cm (2¾ inches) in diameter and leave about five minutes until paste can hold its shape. Tip out and leave to set.

To assemble candlestick:
1. Turn top upside down, position legs, attaching with royal icing, place an icing tube as shown on top and leave to set and thoroughly dry before painting.

2. Spray with quick dry gold enamel paint.
To make candles: See candles page 140 Candles measure 5½ cm (2¼ inches) and 4½ cm (1¾ inches) and about 1½ cm (⅝ inch) thick.
To assemble arrangement:
1. Place candle sticks in position and attach with royal icing to cake.

2. Attach candles to holder with royal icing.

3. Arrange Christmas roses as shown. Add holly leaves and berries.
Flowers required: 3 Christmas roses
                   7 holly leaves
                   9 holly berries (wired and arranged in sets of 3)

Decoration, see page 70
Instructions, see page 73

Stocking Pattern

SANTA'S SLEIGH FILLED WITH PARCELS

Sleigh: See page 71

A delightful sleigh filled with parcels from Santa has been made using a small plastic sleigh as a mould. You will find one such as this in the shops at Christmas time.
Sleigh measures: 8 cm long and 4 cm across the back (3⅛ inches long and 1½ inches across the back).

To make sleigh:
1. Roll out sufficient modelling paste with dowel as finely as practicable and place inside mould which has been cornfloured so paste won't stick. Ease paste into mould with fingers, and when shaped, tip out, neaten around edge with scalpel, replace and allow to set.

2. When thoroughly dry, paint outside with red food coloring.

Runners:
1. Roll a small ball of paste back and forth beneath fingers to a narrow pencil shape (completed runner is length of sleigh). Bend quickly and shape runner as shown and lie flat to dry. Place a pencil either side to hold in position. Make another runner in the same way.

2. Cut two small pieces about 2½ cm x 4 mm (1 inch x ³/₁₆ inch) as finely as practicable. Lie flat and when dry, attach to runners as shown with a little royal icing.
To assemble:
Set sleigh on runners with royal icing and leave to set.
Line sleigh with cotton wool and some finely cut cellophane if you have it. Arrange parcels.

Parcels:
Roll out modelling paste with dowel different thicknesses and cut various shapes. When dry, paint in gay stripes and designs with food colors. A tiny decorated doll adds to the appearance.

CHRISTMAS STOCKING

Completed decoration: See page 71
A Christmas stocking gaily painted and overflowing with parcels makes a novel idea for a Christmas cake. It may be made well in advance and used when required.

1. Cut pattern. · Overall length about 8 cm (3¼ inches)
Heel to toe 9 cm (3½ inches)
Across ankle 5½ cm (2⅛ inches)

2. Using dowel, roll out modelling paste as finely as practicable, place pattern in position and cut out with scalpel.

3. Place a little cotton wool beneath top to give a shallow curve and leave on a flat surface to dry, making sure sides and base are touching surface.

4. When completely set and thoroughly dried out, paint on a bright design with food colors.

5. Place a narrow band of red ribbon around top securing at the back with royal icing.

6. Place stocking on cake attaching at base with royal icing.

7. Place looped and wired red ribbon and a sprig of holly leaves under corner of stocking and arrange parcels, holding into position where they touch with royal icing.

Parcels:
Roll out modelling paste and cut parcels as for sleigh.

THREE WISE MEN

Decoration: See page 70. Pattern opposite.

Three Wise Men bearing gifts of gold, frankincense and myrrh make a striking decoration on a Christmas cake for a religious theme. It would look particularly attractive on an oblong cake made as an open book. Place motifs on one side and a few bars of a Christmas carol on the other side. These motifs were taken from a Christmas card. The outlines are simple and easy to follow.

To make Three Wise Men:
1. Trace and cut out pattern carefully and accurately with small sharp scissors, or obtain similar from a Christmas card.

2. Roll out modelling paste with dowel as finely as practicable, place pattern in position, and carefully cut out with scalpel. Leave flat to dry.

3. Paint as shown in rich purple, red and deep blue with silver and gold. Attach to cake with royal icing.

Top: Cream horn tin used to make modelling paste horn of plenty — instructions see page 123.

CHRISTMAS TREE AND PARCELS

A Christmas tree decorated with colored cashews and surrounded by parcels just waiting to be opened, makes an attractive ornament for a Christmas cake.

To make tree:
1. First make the trunk, which must be set hard before attempting to insert into base, otherwise it will break. Roll a small ball of green modelling paste back and forth beneath finger tips (use both hands) to form a narrow pencil shape about 8½ cm (3¼ inches). Trim each end and leave flat to set.

2. Using firm modelling paste, roll out with dowel, and cut a circle about 2½ cm (1 inch) in diameter and about 3 mm (⅛ inch) thick. Use a small jar if you have one. Mark around edge with the tip of a souvenir spoon handle. Immediately insert trunk into the centre securing with royal icing and leave to dry, making sure it is positioned straight. Use some support if necessary.

3. Use pattern for body of angel, see page 58, and make tree from either modelling paste or green cardboard. If made from modelling paste, leave upright to set.

4. Place a little modelling paste into top of tree, insert trunk securing with a little royal icing. Support if necessary and leave to dry.

5. Holding tree, and using a small leaf tube and firm green royal icing, start at the bottom, and pipe a complete row of leaves to cover the edge, drawing each leaf out as you pipe. Continue in that manner, adding colored cashews with tweezers, until you have completely covered the tree, each row slightly overlapping the previous row.

6. When dry, brush over tree with green food coloring.

7. When dry, brush leaves lightly with a little egg white and sprinkle with glitter.

8. Arrange parcels around tree made from modelling paste as described for Santa's sleigh page 65

A Christmas tree and parcels make a gay and colorful Christmas decoration — instructions above.

Santa Claus, a firm favorite for a Christmas cake — instructions see page 61.

Top: Santa's sleigh filled with parcels — instructions page 65.
Bottom: Christmas stocking — instructions page 65.

HOLLY AND GOLDEN BALLS

Holly leaves, berries and red ribbon have been arranged with graduated balls of paste, threaded onto fine wire and painted gold to make this striking Christmas decoration. It may be made and assembled directly on to cake as shown, or on a plaque.

1. Roll varying sized pieces of firm modelling paste on to the palms of hands to make graduated balls as shown. Leave for a minute or two to firm, so when threaded they won't go out of shape. Take a length of fuse wire about 15 cm (5¾ inches), hook one end, dip in water to stick, and insert into the largest ball. Now thread balls onto wire, graduating them until you have about 11 to 14, varying the number on each of the three wires. Leave to set thoroughly hard for several days. Color with a quick dry gold enamel spray paint.

To assemble on cake:
1. Loop some red ribbon, securing at the base with a short length of flower wire. Twist together the ends of the three strands of wire holding the golden balls, and secure around the base of ribbon.

2. Insert ribbon into cake and arrange holly leaves and berries.

To assemble on plaque:
Make in the same manner as for candy stick, holly and berries below, cutting a circle 11 cm (4½ inches).

CANDY STICK, HOLLY AND BERRIES

This is a simple and colorful Christmas decoration to make. It may be made and assembled directly on cake as shown, or on a plaque.

To make candy stick:
1. Roll a ball of modelling paste back and forth beneath finger tips to a long pencil shape. Cut a length about 19 cm (7½ inches). Trim either end with scalpel, bend quickly to shape and leave flat to dry.

2. Do not bind with ribbon until paste has set hard, otherwise it could break. Starting at one end, attach ribbon at back with a little royal icing. Place a weight on top until royal icing has set, then bind with red ribbon and attach at other end in the same way. Cut ribbon off cleanly at back.
Instructions for Bells, see page 76

Holly leaves:
Roll out modelling paste finely with skewer, and using scalpel, cut out leaves. Place on alfoil to dry, then paint with mixture of green, brown and yellow food coloring to obtain the correct color.

Berries:
Roll small pieces of paste on to palm of hand to form tiny balls. Leave about a

minute, then insert a short length of fine hooked wire into each one, dipping tip of wire first in water to stick. Leave to dry, twist three together to form a spray, hold by wire and paint red.

To assemble on cake:
1. Place candy stick into position securing with royal icing.

2. Insert looped and wired red ribbon.

3. Position bells and leaves, securing with royal icing. Insert holly berries.

To assemble on plaque: (white)
1. Roll out modelling paste with dowel about 3 mm (⅛ inch) thick and cut a circle 10 cm (4 inches) in diameter. Press around the edge firmly with the top of the handle of a souvenir spoon. This will not only thin down the edge, but give an attractive finish.

2. Assemble ornament immediately plaque is made.
   To make bells: See instructions page 76.

LIFT-OFF POSY OF JASMINE AND VIOLETS

Simple to make, this lovely posy of jasmine and violets may be made well in advance, put away, then brought out when the occasion arises.
Flowers required: About 20 jasmine
                   24 jasmine buds
                   18 violets

To make posy:
1. Wire flowers with a long stem about 9 cm (3½ inches), then assemble as though you were arranging a bunch of flowers. Wind a length of cotton around the stems to hold securely, then bind with narrow ribbon as shown.

2. Cut a piece of tulle about 7 cm (2¾ inches) and long enough to give you a slightly gathered circle. Scallop one side, gather straight edge with needle and cotton and draw to fit around posy. Stitch looped ribbon in position.
Lift-off posy of jasmine and violets suitable for a special occasion cake – instructions see page 169

BELLS

Small and large moulded bells can be made from modelling paste, using suitable glasses from Christmas decorations or bought in a shop selling cake-decorating ornaments.

Large bell:
1. Cornflour inside of bell.

2. Roll out modelling paste with dowel about the size of the diameter of the top of the bell and about 5 mm ($^3/_{16}$ inch) thick.

3. Place into bell, and with fingers, ease down towards the base. Keep tipping bell out to make sure paste is not sticking, and with tips of fingers (which have been cornfloured), taper bell as finely as possible towards the edge. Place fingers inside bell, thumb outside, and smooth inside of bell. With your scalpel, keep trimming any surplus paste from around the edge until you have worked the bell as finely as you can.

4. Press the top of a souvenir spoon handle around the edge to give an attractive finish. If you wish, the edge around the bell can be left plain and outlined with a tiny scallop or edged with lace.

5. Finally, tip out to make sure moulded bell has not stuck, replace, and allow to set.

A lovely arrangement suitable for the top tier of a wedding cake of frangipani, snowdrops and hyacinths with a large bell is shown on page 10

Flowers required: 6 frangipani and 5 buds
                      17 snowdrops
                      6 hyacinths
                      5 rose leaves
                      6 snowdrops
                      9 hyacinths.

Bell:
Place a little modelling paste into base of bell, securing with a little water, and wire flowers and loops of ribbon into it. The top of a pearl-tipped stamen has been added around the edge of bell and attached with a dot of royal icing. Two tiny birds positioned at end of ribbon tails complete the arrangement.

Medium size bell:
Make 1 to 3 as for large bell.
4. Tip out to make sure bell has not stuck, replace and allow to set.

Half bells:
1. Make bell in mould as for medium bell.

2. Immediately cut cleanly in half with a scalpel while in the mould. Leave to set.

3. For clapper, roll a piece of paste into a small bell, insert a short length of wire as shown.

ORCHIDS AND LILY-OF-THE-VALLEY

A lovely decoration of green orchids and lily-of-the-valley is shown on page 29 , suitable for a silver wedding anniversary cake.

Embroider bells with a No. OO tube and royal icing in a forget-me-not design. When dry, paint outside of bells and clappers silver.
To elevate bells: Place a little firm modelling paste into top of half bells, attaching with a little water, and insert a piece of flower wire bent into a U shape about 6 cm (2½ inches) into each half bell. Insert into cake.
Flowers required: 2 green orchids tipped in burgundy red
                     9 sprays of lily-of-the-valley (4 back sprays containing
                       6 flowers, other sprays 4 flowers)
                     2 fern

Small bells:
1. Roll out paste about 3 mm (⅛ inch) thick about size of top of bell.

2. Place into bell and work down with fingers. Work out as finely as possible, cutting away any surplus with scalpel.

3. Tip out to make sure bell is not sticking, replace, and leave to set.

4. When completely dry, brush around rim with a little egg white and dip in glitter. Mould a tiny ball of paste, paint red (if required) and attach inside bell with royal icing. See candy stick, holly and bell arrangement page 72

CHRISTMAS TREE – FLAT

This type of Christmas tree can be made very quickly, is easy for a beginner and effective on a small cake.

To make tree:
1. Cut a pattern.

2. Roll out modelling paste with dowel as finely as practicable, place pattern in position, and cut out with scalpel. Leave flat to dry.

3. Complete tree in one of two ways:
(a) Paint tree green (a mixture of brown, green and yellow), shading as shown. Sprinkle on a little glitter while still wet. Leave to dry. Using tweezers, position colored cashews, attaching with a dot of royal icing.
(b) Squeeze a little royal icing over tree with a No. 3 tube, lightly roughing up with a damp brush. Sprinkle lightly with glitter. If you haven't any colored cashews, roll tiny balls of paste, when dry, position on tree with a dot of royal icing. Leave to set, then paint tops only with food coloring in various colors.

Pattern

DECORATED DOLL AND SMALL DOLLS

Decorated cake: See page 146
A bride doll on a birthday cake would appeal to any young girl. Doll measures about 11½ cm (4½ inches) and may be bought in a chain store.

To decorate doll:
1. Cut out skirt and bodice pattern in soft cardboard. Skirt pattern measures 7½ cm (3 inches) – about 1 cm (⅜ inch) longer than doll from waist to hem.

2. Place cardboard skirt around doll, butting seam and join with sticky tape. Tape skirt to body firmly.

3. Using a No. 20 small petal tube and firm royal icing, hold doll upside down, and pipe the first row of petals to cover the edge of the cardboard.

4. Pipe the second row of petals so the top of the petals cover the base of the previous row.

5. Pipe about four rows and sprinkle lightly with glitter. Should you wish to put the doll down, insert feet first into a tumbler.

6. Continue in that manner until the complete skirt has been covered, inserting the head of a pearl-tipped stamen with tweezers as you pipe here and there. Place in tumbler to set.

Bodice:
1. Roll out modelling paste finely, place pattern in position, and cut out with scalpel.

2. Lightly moisten top of doll with a little water, and attach bodice. Immediately position the heads of three pearl-tipped stamens with tweezers down the front of bodice. Leave to set.

3. With a No. 00 tube, pipe loops around bodice edges.

Veil:
1. Cut a piece of tulle about 25 cm long x 19 cm wide (9¾ x 7½ inches). Fold in half and carefully scallop the edges with scissors.

2. Fold lengthways as shown to form two layers of tulle, gather top edge with needle and cotton to fit front of head, leaving about 3½ cm (1⅜ inches) either side.

3. Attach with royal icing and insert three pearl-tipped stamens.

4. Squeeze a little royal icing on to hand, and attach two lengths of ribbon (cut in half) and pearl-tipped stamens to form bouquet. Leave to set.

To decorate doll on cake page 146
Pipe skirt with a No. 20 small petal tube. Pipe a frill from waist to each shoulder

Bodice

Skirt Pattern

81

back and front with a No. 16 leaf tube to form bodice. To make hat, using a small petal tube, start on the outside, and pipe a circle of petals. Working into the centre, pipe several rows of petals to complete.

Small dolls:
Dolls measure 3 cm ($1^3/_{16}$ inch) and are suitable for children's birthday or chistening cakes, they may be bought in a chain store.
1. Hold doll upside down, use a small No. 20 petal tube, and pipe two rows of petals (bottom row first).

2. Pipe lines over the shoulders with a No. 1 tube.

3. If necessary touch up eyes and mouth of doll with food color.

HANDKERCHIEF

A handkerchief from tulle is a lovely idea for an anniversary or Mother's Day cake.

To make handkerchief:
1. Cut out carefully a square of tulle about 20½ cm (8 inches).

2. Fold first in half, and then fold again cutting through four thicknesses, and scallop the edges.

3. Open out, fold almost in half crossways to form a triangle. Lift top fold only, and with fingers pleat two folds either side of the centre. Use pins to hold in position and do not remove until the handkerchief has been embroidered and the royal icing set.

4. Place tulle handkerchief over a dark surface, such as black cardboard to enable you to see the edge clearly. Alternatively, cover a strip of black cardboard with waxed paper, and move it along beneath the edge with one hand as you pipe with the other. Using a No. 00 tube and royal icing of a soft consistency, embroider handkerchief in a simple design.

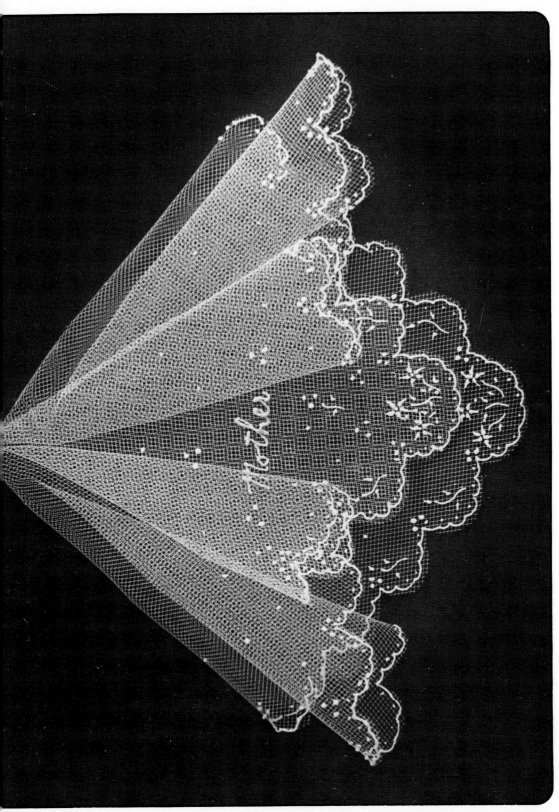

FAN

A lovely decoration suitable for a Mother's Day, anniversary or birthday cake. It is easy to make, but paste must be finely rolled, and it takes time to cut each piece accurately.

Fan measurements: Overall length 14 cm (5½ inches)
Width across top (each piece) 2½ cm (1 inch)
Length base of fan (each piece) 2¼ cm (¾ inch)

Note – it takes 14 pieces to complete fan. The more open the fan, the more pieces will be required.

Method:
1. Roll piece of modelling paste between palms of hands to form a pencil shape. Place on modelling board lightly dusted with cornflour and roll out with skewer as finely as possible.

2. Place pattern in position, and using scalpel, cut out base. With long-bladed knife, cut sides, and using scalpel, shape top.

3. With point of scalpel, carefully cut out slits to allow for threaded ribbon. For obvious reasons, the slits on each piece must be accurately placed.

4. Place each piece as it is cut on to a flat surface and leave until thoroughly set. Do not attempt to thread ribbon until set and dry, otherwise pieces will break. Handle carefully.

To assemble fan:
1. Thread ribbon through the first piece and place in position as shown. Thread the ribbon through the second piece and position so that it just laps at the top. Attach to the base with a little royal icing and firm with fingers. Continue in that manner until all pieces have been threaded. Cut ribbon and secure at back either end with a dot of royal icing. Notice how the pieces form a spiral effect at the base of the fan. Leave to completely set.

2. (a) Using a No. 00 tube, embroider fan as desired.
or
(b) Paint a design on fan with brush and food colors.

3. Roll a small piece of modelling paste finely and cut a handle as shown to fit around fan, securing immediately with a touch of water. Add a dot of royal icing on top. When dry, tip with silver.

4. Loop ribbon as shown and stitch with needle and thread. Insert into opening.

BUTTERFLIES

Butterflies are a dainty addition to a birthday, christening or wedding cake and may be moulded, made in tulle or piped.

Moulded butterflies:
1. Cut a pattern.

2. Roll out a small piece of modelling paste with skewer as finely as possible, place pattern in position, and cut out carefully with scalpel. Cut two, making sure they are a pair and not two for the one side, and shape over a small ball of cotton wool to obtain a shallow curve.

3. When completely dry, paint a design on to one side of the wings and leave to dry. Wings should be so finely moulded that the design can be seen on the other side. When one side has dried, follow the outline, and paint design on the other side. Paste must be thoroughly dried, otherwise color will run. Leave to dry before assembling.

To assemble:
1. With a No. 5 tube and firm royal icing, pipe a small shell, then a long shell to form the body. Pipe directly over long shell a second time.

2. Carefully position wings into body and support with an icing tube either side or a little cotton wool.

3. Cut two stamens about 2½ cm (1 inch), curve over finger, and insert into head as shown. Leave to dry. Attach to cake with royal icing.

Tulle butterflies:
1. Cut a pattern.

2. Fold tulle, pin on pattern, cut out both wings together carefully with tiny scissors. Open out to give you a pair of wings. Place on waxed paper on a dark background so you can easily see tulle to embroider.

3. With a No. 00 tube and soft royal icing, outline and add a touch of embroidery to each wing. For large butterfly, when dry, carefully turn over, and following pipe work, embroider other side of wings for firmness.

4. Assemble in the same way as for moulded butterfly. Handle carefully and make sure pipe work is thoroughly dry before assembling, otherwise it is easily broken.

Piped butterflies: These are very dainty, but I would only recommend that you make them very small as they are fragile.
1. Cut a pattern.

2. Place pattern under waxed paper or greased greaseproof, and using a No. 00 tube, outline pattern. Leave to dry. Pipe extra wings to allow for breakages.

3. Assemble in the same way as for moulded butterflies. Handle carefully.

Butterflies

Moulded

Tulle

Piped

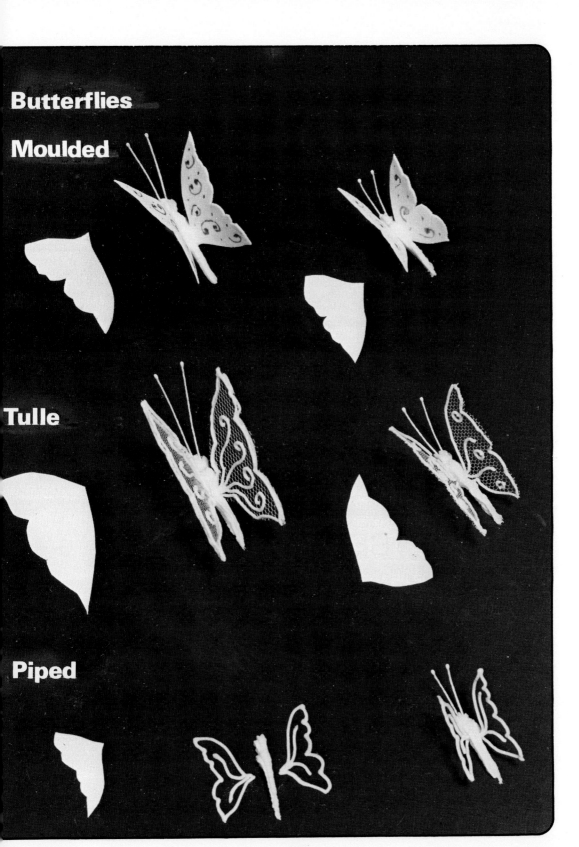

GERANIUMS IN POT

Pattern: See page 22

Pale pink geraniums in a pot make a delightful and novel ornament suitable for a special occasion cake such as a Mother's Day cake.

To make flower pot:
1. Roll out pale green firm modelling paste with dowel as finely as practicable, and cut a strip 3 cm wide (1¼ inches) with a long-bladed knife and long enough to go around a small jar which has been cornfloured on the outside, measuring 3½ cm (1⅜ inches) in diameter, to shape. Place strip around jar, moisten edges with a little water, and butt together to join. Leave to set a few minutes, carefully remove, and leave standing to dry.

2. Roll out modelling paste finely, and cut two narrow strips 5 mm (¼ inch) wide, moisten top and bottom edge of pot with water and attach strips, joining at the back as shown. Leave until thoroughly set.

3. Paint outside green. Leave to dry.
Flowers required: 18 geranium flowers
                      18 buds
                        5 geranium leaves

To assemble:
1. Moisten inside of pot with a little water, insert some firm green modelling paste, making level with the top and filling about the top two-thirds only. Do not pack tightly, **the modelling paste will swell slightly on drying and could burst the pot.** Note – a base is not necessary.

2. Arrange flowers and position leaves with royal icing.

BEER STEIN

Pattern: See page 22
A novel idea for a boy's 21st birthday cake or for dad. It has been painted in red, green, orange and yellow with a horse's head framed in the centre.

Method:
Measurements: Overall height 12½ cm (5 inches)
                    Base 6 cm (2⅜ inches)
1. Cut pattern. See Hints for the Decorator No. 16.

2. Using dowel, roll out modelling paste as finely as practicable, place pattern in position, and cut out carefully with scalpel. Set aside to dry.

3. Roll a small ball of modelling paste back and forth beneath fingers to form handle as shown. Bend quickly to shape and with scalpel, cut each end for a close fit.

4. Before paste has completely set, outline framed horse's head in the centre. See Santa instructions page 61

5. With a ruler and pencil, mark in guidelines for painting colors.

6. When completely set and dry, paint. Allow for one color to dry before painting another color next to it, otherwise color will run.

7. Roll out modelling paste very finely using skewer, and cut out several ivy leaves. Vein with scalpel and leave to dry. Paint.

8. Arrange on cake as shown and using a No. OO tube, pipe greeting. When dry, tip handle of beer stein and writing in gold.
If desired, beer stein may be mounted on a card. Cut card about 9 x 15 cm (3½ x 6 inches) using long-bladed knife. Position beer stein and add a knot ribbon bow on centre of left side of card securing with royal icing.

BOOMERANG AND WILDFLOWER ARRANGEMENT

Pattern of boomerang: See page 131

An arrangement of a boomerang with some Australian wildflowers is a very appropriate ornament suitable for a boy's cake.

To make boomerang: See instructions page 130
Flowers required: 3 sprays Christmas bells (4 or 5 flowers and
3 buds to each spray)
3 sprays wattle
3 sprays brown boronia (3 flowers to each spray)
3 maidenhair fern

To assemble ornament:
1. Knead a little brown food coloring into modelling paste.

2. Cut out plaque – an 8½ cm circle (3¼ inches). See pattern posy of spring flowers page 23

3. Place loops of green ribbon at back and arrange wildflowers as shown.

4. Rest boomerang across arrangement. Leave on flat surface to thoroughly dry. Once paste has set, flowers will be firmly positioned.

Top: Boomerang and wildflower arrangement
suitable for a boy's cake — instructions above.
Bottom: Horseshoe for a boy's 21st —
instructions page 128.

SAILING SCENE

Sailing scene: See page 90
Pattern opposite.
Shells: See below
Sailing ships, lighthouse and shells have been used to create a scene suitable for a masculine cake.

To make lighthouse:
1. Cut pattern.

2. Roll out modelling paste with dowel as finely as practicable, place pattern in position, and cut out with scalpel. Leave to completely set before painting with food colors.

To make sailing boats:
Cut a pattern and cut out as for lighthouse. Notice the small V at the base of sailing boat to enable you to attach to cake.
Shells were gathered along the shore. Open shells are easily made as they can be used as a mould. Other shells shown will depend on the decorator's skill.

To mould open shells:
1. Roll out a small ball of modelling paste very finely with skewer, and press over the outside of shell which has been cornfloured, to obtain markings.

2. Tip out, and trim around the edge with a scalpel.

3. Replace over shell to set. When dry, paint.

To assemble scene:
1. Cover cake with fondant (white).

2. Brush over foreground with a little egg white and sprinkle with lemon jelly crystals.

3. Place lighthouse in position, attaching with royal icing.

4. Paint in water and sky.

5. Position sailing boats by inserting V into cake covering.

6. Arrange shells and paint steps and railing of lighthouse directly on to cake. Brush a little green around base of lighthouse.

Maidenhair Fern:
Twist together three lengths of fuse wire or fine flower wire and place on waxed paper, making sure wires are flat on surface. Using a No. 0 tube, pipe dots along wires, leave about 30 seconds, dip tip of forefinger in cornflour and flatten. Leave to dry, paint a soft green.

Fishbone Fern:
Twist wire as for maidenhair fern. Pipe dots along either side of wires with a squeeze and pull motion. Leave to dry, paint a soft green.

ghthouse Pattern   **Sailing Boat Pattern**

1   **2**

Fishbone Fern

2.Maidenhair Fern

BON VOYAGE CARD – SHIP

See page: 109

A novel idea for a farewell cake to friends who may be going away on a holiday by ship. This idea was obtained from a card. It would also be suitable for a masculine birthday cake. Card measurements: 17 x 11½ cm (6¾ x 4½ inches).

1. Roll out modelling paste with dowel as finely as practicable. To save cutting a pattern, use a card to ensure straight sides, place in position and cut out with long-bladed knife.

2. To transfer ship on to modelling paste, follow instructions given in detail for Santa Claus 1 to 4 page 61

3. Leave to completely dry before attempting to paint with food colors, making sure one color is dry before painting another color next to it.

4. A little royal icing has been roughed up around bow of boat and sprinkled with glitter while still wet.

5. Pipe writing with a No. 00 tube, tip when dry. Add bow, attaching with royal icing.
Note – ship can also be made in modelling paste. Roll out paste finely, cut out and attach to card with a little water. Paint when dry.

Moulded shells — instructions see page 94.

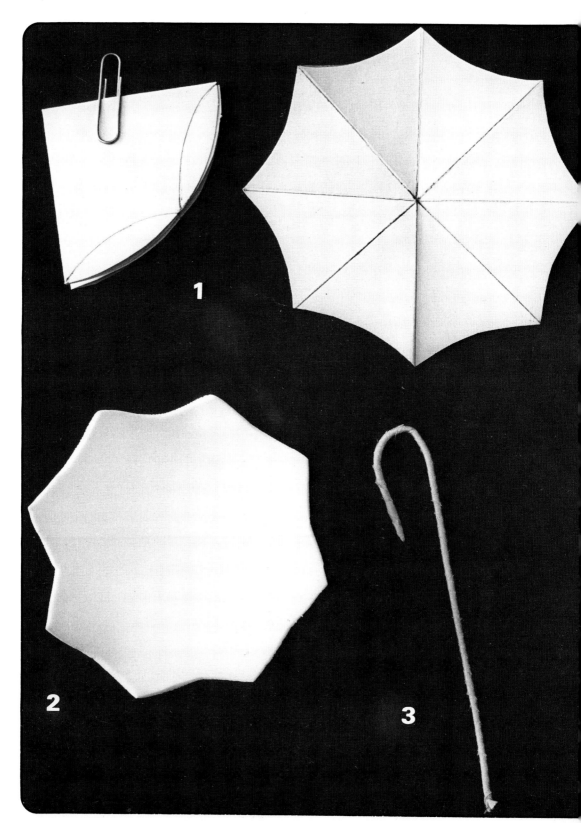

1

2

3

OPEN UMBRELLA

Oranament: See page 31
An open umbrella filled with roses would look lovely on a birthday, Mother's Day or a wedding cake.

Flowers required: 6 single roses
                          about 3 doz. small flowers
                          4 rose leaves

To make umbrella: Mould in color if desired.

1. Cut a pattern – a circle 11½ cm (4½ inches) in diameter. To cut a quick and accurate pattern, turn a bowl upside down, outline onto paper, and cut out. Fold circle in half, open out and fold each half in half (4 sections). Open out and fold through the centre of each section (8 sections). Fold carefully back into four sections, and cutting through four thicknesses, cut two scallops as shown. Open out to form shape of umbrella.

2. Roll out modelling paste with dowel as finely as practicable, place pattern in position, and cut out with scalpel. Place inside a bowl to shape without pleating and leave to set.

3. Bind a pipe cleaner or several thicknesses of wire 16 cm (6¼ inches long) with satin ribbon. Bend to form handle.

To assemble:

1. As it would take a large amount of modelling paste to fill umbrella, place some cotton wool in base first, then add modelling paste so that it is smooth on top, rounded in the centre and tapering to the edge. Moisten with water around inside of edge to stick.

2. Position handle in centre. Insert several pieces of wired tulle and loops of ribbon to soften the arrangement (to make, see posy of spring flowers page 23).

3. Attach roses and leaves with royal icing and arrange small flowers.

4. Attach ribbon bow to handle. Leave to set.

Flowers required: 6 roses
                          about 3 doz small flowers
                          5 leaves.

FLOWER CART

Ornament: See page 111

A flower cart filled with jasmine and forget-me-nots would make an ideal orna-ment for a 21st birthday cake. It can also be outlined directly onto cake covering and flowers arranged into icing.

Make the plaque in plastic icing (the same as the cake covering) as the icing must be set sufficiently before tracing on the pattern. If made in modelling paste, by the time the piping was completed, the icing would have set, and you would not be able to wire in the flowers.

Flowers must be made and painted and ready when required.

Flowers required: 12 jasmine
                      12 jasmine buds
                      18 moulded forget-me-nots in pink, blue, mauve and lemon

To make flower cart:

1. Cut an oval pattern 13½ x 11½ cm (5¼ x 4½ inches). See Hints for the Decorator No. 16.

2. Knead green color into icing which can be a contrasting color to the cake, roll out with dowel, place pattern in position and cut shape.

3. Mark around edge with top of a souvenir spoon handle for an attractive finish.

4. Trace cart pattern.

5. When icing has set firmly, place tracing on plaque and using a pencil, outline tracing on to icing. If you wish, lightly pencil in markings, and using a No. 1 tube, outline barrow and wheels. A No. 00 tube is used for other pipe work.

6. When dry, paint barrow, umbrella handle and top brown, and umbrella green.

7. Arrange flowers. Leave flat to set.

WATERING CAN

Ornament: See page 111

A watering can filled with flowers makes a novel and attractive ornament suitable for a birthday, anniversary or Mother's Day cake. It has been set on a plaque so it may be removed and kept, but may be also arranged directly onto the cake if you wish.

Tiny flowers only are suitable for an arrangement such as this, and I have chosen apricot roses and hyacinths and forget-me-nots in blue, mauve, lemon and orange.

Flowers required: 6 roses
                      3 buds
                      8 hyacinths
                   15 forget-me-nots in various colors
                    3 single stems maidenhair fern

Loops of green ribbon which has been cut in half for a dainty appearance.

Watering Can

Pattern

ower Cart

Pattern

Note – all flowers must be moulded and painted ready to arrange immediately plaque has been cut out.

To make watering can:
Measurements: Overall height 8 cm (3⅛ inches)
                        Width at base 4½ cm (1¾ inches)
                        Width across top 6½ cm (2½ inches)

1. Cut pattern.

2. Using dowel, roll out modelling paste in pale green as finely as practicable, place pattern in position and cut out.

3. Place a little cotton wool beneath top as shown and leave to set, making sure sides and base are touching surface.

4. To make handle: Roll out modelling paste very finely and cut a narrow strip using long-bladed knife, about 23 cm (9 inches). Curl each end quickly around a paint brush handle, shape as shown and leave to set. Tip top edge gold.

5. Paint design on watering can with food colors. Note – the two bands with painted design have been left the original pale green background.

Plaque:
1. Knead a little lemon food coloring into sufficient paste to cut a circle about 12½ cm (5 inches) and 3 mm (⅛ inch) thick. Use dowel to roll out.

2. Mark around edge with top of a souvenir spoon handle.

3. Position watering can and handle on plaque securing with royal icing and immediately wire flowers and loops of ribbon into base before paste sets. If you wish, you can make the plaque from plastic icing which will allow more time to arrange the flowers.

Lovely floral arrangement with bucket of champagne suitable for a golden wedding anniversary cake — instructions see page 104.

RECORD

A record is very appropriate for a boy's 21st birthday cake.

To make record: Measurement 11 cm (4½ inches) in diameter. Make it any size you wish. Use anything you have on hand to cut the various size circles, such as tops of glasses, bowls, lids from screw-top jars or similar.

1. Cut patterns in various sizes as shown.

2. Roll out modelling paste with dowel as finely as practicable, place largest pattern in position and cut out with scalpel. Smooth around edge with finger and cut a small hole in the centre.

3. Place next size in position, and lightly mark around edge with scalpel. Mark all the circles in that manner, lightly marking also in between circles freehand with scalpel to give the effect.
Leave flat to dry.

4. Paint with artists' black water color.

5. Roll out paste finely, and cut a small circle about 3 cm (1¼ inches), also a small hole in the centre. Moisten back with a little water, and position in the centre as shown. Leave to dry.

6. With a No. 00 tube, pipe greeting, and when dry, tip gold.

Moulded key:
1. Roll modelling paste out finely with skewer, press a door key firmly on to paste (which has been cornfloured) so the markings will show, and cut out carefully with scalpel. Leave flat to dry.

2. Paint gold. Position on to record with royal icing.

BUCKET OF CHAMPAGNE

A bucket of champagne tipped in gold and arranged with a lovely spray of roses, jasmine, Michaelmas daisies and hyacinths, is a novel idea for a golden wedding anniversary celebration.
Flowers required: 3 roses
                    18 jasmine flowers and 18 buds
                     6 Michaelmas daisies
                     8 hyacinths
                     4 rose leaves

To make bucket of champagne:
1. Cut a pattern.

2. Roll out modelling paste with dowel as finely as practicable, place pattern in position and cut out with scalpel. Leave flat to dry.

3. Pipe embroidery with a No. 00 tube, 50 with a No. 3 tube. When dry, paint gold, leaving ice white.

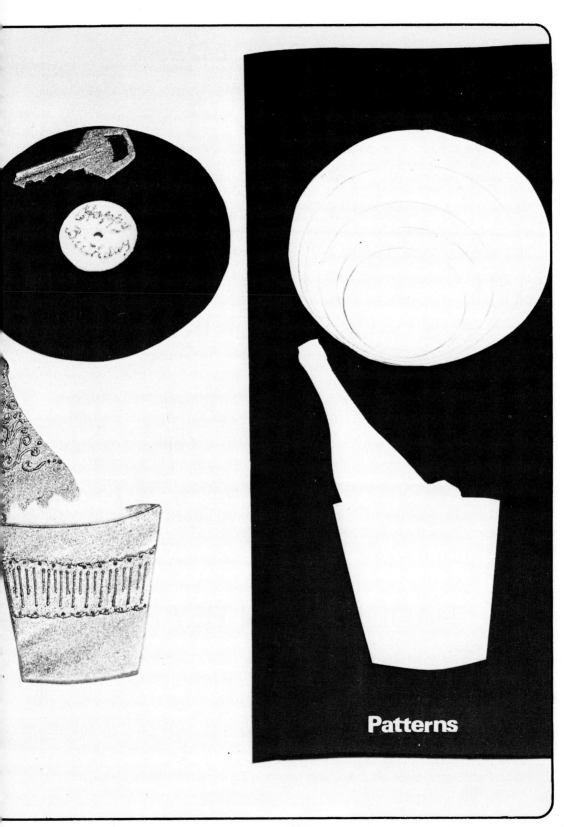

Patterns

VINTAGE CAR

A vintage car set on a plaque is very easily made and suitable for a boy's birthday cake.

To make vintage car:
1. Select a card at a newsagent's that is clear and easy for you to trace.

2. Plaque measures 10 x 7½ cm (4 x 3 inches). Cut plaque large enough to take pattern of car. Roll out modelling paste in white with dowel as finely as practicable, and cut out plaque with long-bladed knife.

3. To transfer vintage car on to plaque, follow the instructions given in detail for Santa Claus page 61 from 1 to 4.

4. Paint.

STACKED BOOKS

An idea such as this would be suitable to celebrate the passing of an examination.
Measurements for stacked books vary from:
8 cm length and 2 cm depth (3⅛ inches length and ¾ inch depth) at the base to:
5¼ cm length and 1½ cm depth (2¼ inches length and ⅝ inch depth) at the top.

1. Cut a pattern as shown, cutting carefully and accurately.

2. Roll out modelling paste with dowel about 3 mm (⅛ inch) thick, place pattern in position, and cut out with scalpel. Leave flat to dry.

3. When completely dry, paint covers in red, green, yellow and brown, making sure one color is dry before painting another color next to it. Paint leaves of books gold.
Gnome: (optional) Cut out tiny gnome in the same manner, very finely. Paint when dry.

PADDINGTON BEAR

See page: 109
Paddington Bear, a favorite with young children,. would make a delightful cake decoration. The pattern was obtained from a birthday card which can be bought at any newsagent.
Follow the instructions given in detail for Santa Claus page 61 from 1 to 4.
5. When thoroughly dry, paint with food colors of your choice. The shine on the shoes and hat has been obtained by simply removing some of the color with a damp brush. Don't forget, allow each color to dry before painting next to it. Refer constantly to your original card for shading.
Place Paddington bear on cake, and brush in foreground and sky with food colors. When dry, paint railing.

MOTIFS FOR CHILDREN'S CAKES

Motifs such as these may be obtained from birthday cards, story books or gift wrapping paper and are suitable for children's cakes. They may be made well in advance and keep indefinitely if stored in a dry place. Use dowel to roll out large motifs and skewer for small motifs.

1. Dog and cat: Cut a pattern. Roll out modelling paste as finely as practicable, place pattern in position, and careully cut out with scalpel. Leave flat to dry. Paint with food colors, painting first the background color. Leave to completely dry before painting in detail. To set off motifs, brush a little food color in soft green and brown around base.

2. Lamb: This has been made with a combination of modelling paste and royal icing. Make as for 1. When modelling paste has dried, with a No. 3 tube, squeeze firm royal icing over lamb, and working in sections, rough up with a slightly damp brush to give a woolly effect. When completely dry, paint in detail and place a pink ribbon bow around neck, attaching with royal icing. Tiny bow is made in the same way as moulded bootees page 54 Paint sprigs of grass and forget-me-nots directly on to cake with brush or pipe with a No. 00 tube and royal icing, and touch up when dry.

3. Teddy bears: Make as for 1. Motifs such as teddy bears, rabbits, ducks and similar may be positioned around the sides of a cake securing with royal icing when completed.

4. Chickens: Make as for 1. Feet and grass are either painted directly on to cake or piped as in 2.

5. Soldiers: These would delight any small boy on his birthday cake. Make as for 1. When cutting out, cut a small V into the bottom, which is set into a base when dry. When soldiers have been painted and dry, cut a small base about 2½ cm (1 inch) circle. Mark around edge with tip of a souvenir spoon handle and insert soldier into base, securing with a little royal icing. Support until set.

6. Dog: Make as for 1. Position on cake with royal icing and paint brown and green food color for a background as shown.

7. Easter bunny: Make your own Easter bunny and attach to a plain chocolate egg for a gift at Easter. A similar motif will be found on an Easter card. Make as for 1 and attach to egg with royal icing.

8. Rabbits: Suitable for a christening cake. Make as for 1. Pipe grass and forget-me-knots and tip when dry or paint with food coloring directly on to cake.

9. Ducks: Make as for 1. Motifs were found in a child's story book. Brush a little blue food coloring around ducks for effect.

Flower cart filled with flowers — a delightful ornament for a birthday cake — instructions see page 100.
Watering can filled with roses, hyacinths and forget-me-nots makes a novel ornament for a special occasion cake — instructions see page 100.

BASKETS OF FLOWERS

Red roses and snowdrops (top) combine to make a pretty basket suitable for a Mother's Day or birthday cake and may be removed and kept almost indefinitely.

Method: See instructions wedding vase page 38
For basket, leave off base and bind either several thicknesses of your flower wire or a pipe cleaner with narrow satin ribbon, securing with needle and cotton to make the handle.
Position handle and arrange flowers immediately modelling paste has been placed in basket.
Flowers required: 12 roses
                      18 snowdrops
                      3 maidenhair fern
Basket of sweet peas and hyacinths (bottom) is suitable for a birthday, anniversary or the top tier of a wedding cake.
To make basket: Roll out modelling paste as finely as practicable and cut a circle about 10 cm (4 inches). Press end of souvenir spoon handle around the edge which becomes the outside of basket. Curve to shape sides as shown and place some support either side until set.
Complete basket in the same manner as for red roses and snowdrops.
Flowers required: 2 sprays apricot sweet peas (each spray containing 5 flowers and a bud)
                      3 sprays mauve sweet peas (each spray containing 3 flowers and a bud)
                      6 sprays mauve hyacinths (each spray containing 3 flowers and a bud)
                      4 maidenhair fern
Sweet pea tendrils have been made by winding cotton-covered wire around a needle, then painting with green food coloring.

SWANS

A lovely swan suitable for a christening cake can be made using a plastic swan as a pattern. It may be bought in a shop selling cake-decorating ornaments.

Method:
1. Shape head and neck. Roll a ball of paste back and forth with fingertips until length required. Bend to shape exactly as in plastic swan. With thumb and forefinger flatten tip to form beak, shape head and with scalpel trim other end as shown. Lie flat to completely set.

2. Place plastic swan on paper and outline base. Cut pattern. Roll out paste about 6 mm (¼ inch) thick, place pattern in position and cut out base, and immediately position swan's neck into base, securing with a little royal icing. **Note** – this must be completely set and dry, otherwise it will break when handling. Support if necessary, and leave to set, making sure to set at the same angle as plastic swan.

3. Cut pattern for wing. It might be necessary to make several wings in modelling paste before you obtain an accurate pattern. Roll out modelling paste finely and cut out with scalpel. Place over outside of plastic wing which has been cornfloured so paste won't stick, and firmly press all over with fingers to obtain markings on wing. Remove, place on board, and using scalpel, nick as shown around top of wing.

4. By this time wing should be setting and holding the shape. Moisten side of base and position wing so that markings are on the outside. Make another wing in the same manner. If necessary, place a little cotton wool into the centre until wings have set.

5. Paint beak, mark in eyes. Cut a selvedge of ribbon long enough to trail attractively, and attach under beak with a little royal icing.

There are several ways of presenting the swan:
1. See page . . . Place swan on cake and brush a little blue food coloring around swan as shown. Place a tiny decorated doll (on cotton wool if necessary) in back of swan and a little pair of moulded shoes at end of trail of ribbon.

2. Place a little modelling paste into back of swan and fill with tiny flowers such as rosebuds, hyacinths, snowdrops, bouvardia, forget-me-nots, and karume azaleas.

3. Trail a few tiny flowers such as apple blossom from ends of ribbon.

Tiny swans: These can make a dainty decoration on a christening cake. See swan christening cake page 166

To mould swans:
1. Take a small ball of modelling paste, draw out in one place with fingers and swivel until length required for neck.

2. Quickly bend to shape neck and flatten tip between thumb and forefinger.

3. With fingers pinch up sides and back to form wings and tail, and mark with scalpel. Stand upright and leave to dry. Tip beak yellow and a dot of black for eyes. Position on cake with a little royal icing. Alternatively: After 2, stand in upright position and leave to dry. Roll out modelling paste very finely and cut two tiny wings and a tail and attach to body with a little water.

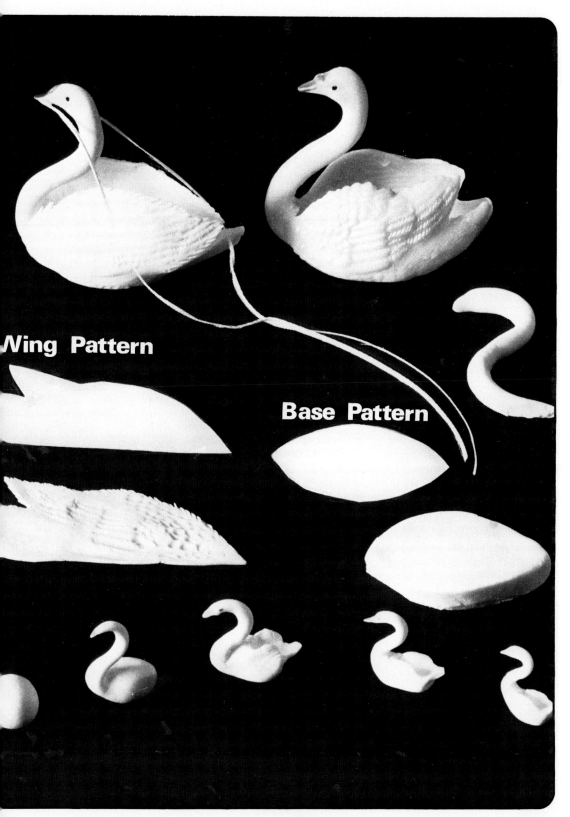

Wing Pattern

Base Pattern

JASMINE AND VIOLETS IN GOLD VASE

A lift-off ornament of jasmine and violets arranged in a gold vase would make a lovely decoration for a birthday, anniversary or Mother's Day cake.

To make vase:
1. Cut pattern: Overall length 8 cm (3 inches)
Base 3.5 cm (1¾ inches)
Width at top about 4 cm (1½ inches)
Width at centre 22 mm (⅞ inch)
To cut an accurate pattern, see Hints for the Decorator 16.

2. Roll out modelling paste as finely as practicable, place pattern in position and carefully cut out with scalpel. Press an edging at top of vase if desired with top of souvenir spoon handle. Place a little cotton wool under top edge as shown and leave to set.

3. Paint gold.
Plaque: Roll out firm modelling paste (pastel green), and cut out with scalpel a circle 12 cm in diameter (4¾ inches). Press souvenir spoon handle around edge to give a scalloped finish and leave to dry.

To assemble:
1. Position vase, attaching at base with royal icing.

2. Place a little modelling paste into top of vase (moisten to stick), attach violet leaves to plaque with royal icing and immediately arrange flowers with some loops of green ribbon. Loop ribbon, securing at base with a twist of wire.
Flowers required: 10 jasmine flowers
13 jasmine buds
8 violets
3 leaves

Pattern

Pattern

CONFIRMATION ORNAMENT

A small plaque embroidered with sheafs of wheat and a chalice to represent bread and wine has been surrounded with lilies, hyacinths and lily-of-the-valley and mounted on a larger plaque to make this attractive confirmation ornament.

Flowers required: 6 lilies
18 white hyacinths
2 sprays lily-of-the-valley
3 sprays maidenhair fern

To make small plaque:

1. Cut a pattern about 9 x 6 cm (3½ x 2⅜ inches) as shown.

2. Roll out modelling paste with dowel as finely as practicable, place pattern in position, and cut out with long-bladed knife. Press a tiny cross immediately into paste to mark, or pipe a cross on later. Leave flat to dry.

3. Cut out chalice and circle (bread) about 1.3 cm in diameter from modelling paste rolled out very finely.

4. When dry, attach to small plaque with royal icing.

5. Using a No. 00 tube, pipe a snail's trail around edge of plaque and pipe sheafs of wheat.

6. When dry, tip chalice, cross and wheat, gold.

Large plaque:

1. Roll out modelling paste in the same manner and cut out a plaque about 14 x 10 cm (5½ x 4 inches). Leave flat to dry.

2. Outline with a tiny scallop using a No. 00 tube and royal icing.

3. Place a banana-shaped piece of paste on to plaque (moisten with water to stick), and wire flowers into it, together with looped ribbon and a little tulle. It also supports the small plaque and should not be seen when ornament is completed. Secure small plaque with a little royal icing along the base.

ORANGE BLOSSOM SHELL

A beautiful ornament filled with orange blossom and hyacinths and suitable for the top tier of a wedding cake has been made using a scallop shell off the beach as a mould. I have shown the complete scallop shell, but as it may not always be possible to obtain the top, I have made the ornament using the bottom half. It would also be possible to buy a shell at a beach resort. This idea could be used on a birthday or anniversary cake filled with suitable flowers such as fuchsias, daffodils, jonquils, Cecil Brunner roses or similar.

Method:
1. Mould in white for a wedding cake and in a pastel shade if desired for a celebration cake. Using dowel, roll out modelling paste as finely as practicable, place in shell which has been cornfloured so paste won't stick, and firmly press over entire surface to transfer pattern on to paste.

2. Tip out on to board, and with scalpel, cut carefully around marked edge. Replace in shell and leave to set. When shell has set sufficiently, tip out and made the other half in the same way.

To assemble:
1. Place just sufficient modelling paste into base towards the back of shell (moisten to stick) to secure flowers and attach lid.

2. Immediately arrange flowers with loops of narrow white ribbon (cut in half). Position top half of shell firmly into paste, securing if necessary with royal icing.
Flowers required: 18 orange blossom
                                6 orange blossom buds
                                12 hyacinths

DOLL IN ROSE

A tiny decorated doll in the centre of a full blown rose is a lovely idea for a christening cake ornament. If desired, it may be mounted on a plaque, removed and kept.

Method:
1. Mould petals for a full blown rose in the usual way.

2. When assembling, place a tiny decorated doll in the centre instead of stamens.

3. Attach rose and leaves to cake with a little royal icing. Place wired tulle and loops of ribbon behind rose to complete the decoration.

4. Alternatively, mount on plaque. Roll out modelling paste as finely as practicable and cut a circle about 9 cm (3½ inches). To obtain an attractive finish, mark around edge with top of souvenir spoon handle and immediately arrange decoration.

MARZIPAN FRUITS AND VEGETABLES

Marzipan Fruits: See below   Vegetables: See page 124

It is usual for moulded fruits and vegetables to be made in marzipan. If you don't like marzipan, there is no reason why they can't be made from plastic fondant used for covering the cake, with a little flavoring added. If they are intended to be used as ornaments and not to be eaten, then they could be made in modelling paste. It is a good idea to mould all fruits and vegetables in modelling paste while in season, paint, pack away and keep as a sample, as they will keep indefinitely. For best results, mould fruits and vegetables untinted, leave at least one day to thoroughly set before painting in food colors.

I am giving you a variety of fruits and vegetables to make, but of course, there are a great many more you could make. To make moulded fruits and vegetables appear as life-like as possible, real ones should be used as models.

MARZIPAN FRUITS:

Pineapple:
Mould about six tiny leaves in modelling paste and leave to dry. Mould pineapple to shape, mark outside with scalpel in a diamond effect, and with point of tweezers, pinch each section for realism. Immediately insert tiny leaves into top and leave to set. Paint orange with a touch of brown, and a little green to show it is not completely ripe.

Pear:
Mould to shape by rolling into a ball and taper towards the top. Insert the head of a clove in the bottom and the stem in the top, which will also help to shape the fruit. Brush all over in pastel yellow and add a soft touch of red to give a blush to one side. Make some green for variation.

Apple:
Mould to shape, inserting clove the same as for pear. Paint a soft green, or have some rosy with a touch of green and yellow.

Orange:
Mould into a ball, roll over the second smallest hole in the grater to give the correct appearance of an orange. Paint orange.

Lemon:
Mould into an oval and mark as for orange. Paint yellow with a touch of green.

Peach:
Mould to shape. With modelling stick, press down one side and slightly groove the piece of fruit. Brush first all over in yellow, and while still wet, brush a little red through to give a blush on the fruit.

Apricot:
Mould to shape, complete as for peach, making fruit smaller. Brush all over with apricot food coloring, and while still wet, add a shading of green to some pieces to indicate fruit has not ripened.

Plum:
Mould to shape, complete as for peach. Paint either purple or green.

Banana:
Mould to shape. Paint yellow with some brown markings usually seen on bananas. Touch up both ends brown, and add a touch of green to some to show fruit is not quite ripe.

Grapes:
Mould into small ovals. Attach with a little egg white to stick, and build up until you have a bunch (about 13). Leave to set. Paint green or purple.

Cherries:
Make tiny stalks from modelling paste. Roll very tiny pieces of paste between fingers to form a fine stalk. Leave to set hard, and insert into cherry on completion. Cherries – roll into small balls, insert stalk, paint red, and stalk green.

Strawberries:
Mould to shape. Brush over with burgundy red food color, and roll in crystal sugar.

HORN OF PLENTY

Fruit tumbling from a horn of plenty makes a colorful decoration for a boy's cake. Fruit alone, arranged attractively, is eye-catching.

Horn of plenty can be made in one of two ways.

Method 1: Photograph page 67. Horn can be finely moulded. Use a cream horn tin, which may be bought at a hardware store, as a mould.

1. Knead a little brown food coloring into the modelling paste.

2. Roll out modelling paste with dowel as finely as practicable, place around cream horn tin which has been cornfloured, cut with scalpel to fit, and join down the back with a little water where it won't be seen.

3. Trim around top edge with scissors or scalpel, and taper with fingers down the base and curve as shown. Leave to set. Remove, paint brown.

Method 2: See page 91 Measures 11 cm long (4½ inches) and 5½ cm (2¼ inches) across the top.

It is not as easy to make or as finely moulded as method 1, and it will depend on your ability to handle a large piece of paste, which should be of a soft consistency to enable you to work it without too much cracking.

1. Work into a cone, and start to hollow with fingers. Place your fingers inside and thumb outside, and smooth the inside as much as you can. You won't be able to avoid some cracking on the outside. Taper with fingers down the base and curve as shown. By this time, it should be quite firm and already setting. Stand upright and leave to thoroughly set.

2. Basket weave over horn with a No. 5 tube and royal icing, adding a little brown food coloring.

3. When set, paint with brown food coloring.

To arrange decoration:
Place horn of plenty in position on cake securing with royal icing. Tumble fruits from horn as shown, attaching with royal icing where necessary. A few moulded peach leaves give added interest.

MARZIPAN VEGETABLES:

A wheelbarrow filled with marzipan vegetables would make a novel birthday surprise for dad. Make a little larger if desired, line with alfoil or waxed paper, and fill with sweets or nuts and use as a table decoration for Christmas or a birthday celebration.

Pattern: See page 129   Wheelbarrow with vegetables: See page 110
Measurements: Across front   4 cm (1½ inches)
              Depth   6 cm (2½ inches)
              Across back   6 cm (2½ inches)

To make wheelbarrow:
1. Cut a pattern as shown in cardboard firm enough when assembled to hold modelling paste wheelbarrow to set. Cut a small V from each corner. Secure with sticky tape.

2. Roll out modelling paste with dowel as finely as practicable, place pattern in position, and carefully cut out with scalpel.
Place in mould to set.

3. Handles: Make two.
Roll a ball of modelling paste back and forth beneath fingers into a long pencil shape, and cut a length 14 cm (5½ inches). Cut one end as shown with scalpel and slightly curve to shape, and make a hole through the other end with a match.

4. Wheel:
Roll out modelling paste with dowel, and cut a circle 2½ cm (1 inch) and 3 mm (⅛ inch) as shown. Make a hole through the centre with a match. Leave flat to dry.

5. Legs: Cut two.
Roll out modelling paste with dowel and cut two strips 2½ cm (1 inch) long x 1 cm (⅜ inch) wide and 3 mm (⅛ inch) thick. Leave flat to set.

To assemble:
1. Turn barrow upside down. Position wheel between two handles and insert match (length required). Secure handles with royal icing.

2. Attach legs on outside of handles with royal icing. If necessary, squeeze a little royal icing into joins at corners and smooth off with a damp brush.

3. Paint brown.

Cabbage: In wheelbarrow.
Mould paste into a ball to form the centre. Shape about eight leaves gradually increasing in size and attach to centre with a touch of egg white, each one overlapping the previous one. Paint green:

Top row left to right:

Half watermelon:
I have added watermelon in wheelbarrow vegetable display to give color, there-
fore it is included in vegetable instructions. Mould into an oval, and with long-
bladed knife cut lengthways through the centre. Paint outside green, leave a
narrow strip, and paint the centre a deep pink. When dry, paint seeds brown.

Slice of watermelon:
Mould into a strip and cut a half circle. Paint as above.

Cauliflower:
Mould centre with fondant icing. Shape into a ball to form the centre and roll top
across the second smallest holes in grater to give a natural appearance.
Complete as for cabbage.

Squash:
Mould into a circular shape, and with modelling stick, press around edge to give
indentations as shown. Paint light green, with a little brown brushed through.

Open pod with peas:
Shape open pod. Mould about six tiny peas. Paint green, and place in pod.

Peas:
Mould about six peas. Shape open pod, place peas along the centre and fold
over. Press to join. Paint green.

Middle row:

Celery:
Roll marzipan beneath finger tip to form a long slim shape, and press lengthways
around a pencil to shape, pressing out with finger tips at the base. Dilute green
food coloring to a pastel shade, painting deeper green towards the top and paler
towards the base.

Potato:
Mould into various potato shapes. Pierce in several places with pointed end of
modelling stick to represent the eyes, and paint brown.

Tomato:
Mould to shape. Paint red, with a touch of green.

Pumpkin:
Mould into a ball. Indent slightly on top with the rounded end of modelling stick,
also the side from the centre to the base in several places. Paint green, and
while still wet, brush a little brown lightly through.

Piece of pumpkin:
Mould into a ball and cut out a wedge with knife. Paint outside green, inside a
soft orange/yellow.

Bottom row:

Bean:
Mould to shape. Point one end with fingers and draw a small stalk out with
fingers at the other end. Paint green.

Carrot:
Roll into a pencil shape, wider at one end and tapering to a point. Paint orange and mark in several places across the carrot with touches of brown.

Parsnip:
Mould as for carrot. Dilute a little yellow food coloring and paint parsnips a cream color. Mark as for carrot.

Cucumber:
Mould to shape. Using tweezers, pinch here and there over the surface for a natural appearance. Paint green and a touch of yellow.

Onion:
Mould to shape. Paint brown.

BIRD FOUNTAIN

A bird fountain is shown to advantage with Michaelmas daisies and hyacinths, and makes a lovely ornament for the top of a wedding cake.

To make bird fountain:
1. Base: First make the stem. Roll a small ball of modelling paste beneath fingers to form a pencil shape and cut a length with scalpel about 2½cm (1 inch) as shown, leave to completely set. Roll out modelling paste about 4mm ($^3/_{16}$ inch) thick with dowel, and cut a circle 2½cm (1 inch) in diameter. Press the tip of a souvenir spoon handle around the edge and immediately position stem as shown, securing with royal icing. If necessary, support until completely set. Cut another circle the same and position in the same manner. It will be easier to set the second circle, if it is placed on the bottom to set.

2. Top: Use a dish similar to one shown, which may be bought at a hardware store. Make exactly as for wedding cake vase page 38

3. When completely dry, attach to base with royal icing and leave to set. Four tiny birds, tipped silver, have been placed around edge of fountain and attached with royal icing after flowers have been arranged.
Flowers required: 12 Michaelmas daisies
20 hyacinths and 6 buds
Only a selvedge of the ribbon has been used to give a dainty appearance.

HORSESHOE FOR A BOY'S 21ST

Ornament: See page 92

An attractive ornament can be made with some Australian wildflowers and a horseshoe to add congratulations.

Flowers required: 5 flannel flowers
2 sprays pink boronia (3 flowers to each spray)
3 sprays gumnuts
2 sprays wattle
1 spray Christmas bush (3 flowers to spray)

To make horseshoe: Mould in color (green).
1. Cut a pattern.

2. Roll out modelling paste with dowel as finely as practicable, place pattern in position, and cut out carefully with scalpel. Smooth around edge with fingers or mark around edge with the top of a souvenir spoon handle as shown. Leave flat to dry.

3. Pipe a key with a No. 3 tube on to waxed paper, pipe congratulations on horseshoe with a No. 00 tube, and when dry, tip in gold.

To assemble: Set on a plaque (cream).
1. Roll out firm modelling paste in color with dowel, allowing some thickness to enable you to arrange the flowers, and cut a circle about 11 cm (4½ inches).

2. Press the top of a souvenir spoon handle around the edge. This will not only give the ornament an attractive finish, but will thin the plaque around the edge.

3. Immediately arrange flowers with loops of green ribbon. Support horseshoe as shown on flowers. Attach key with royal icing.

Photo shows in detail how to make wheelbarrow
— instructions see page 124.
Pattern of horseshoe for a masculine cake —
instructions above.

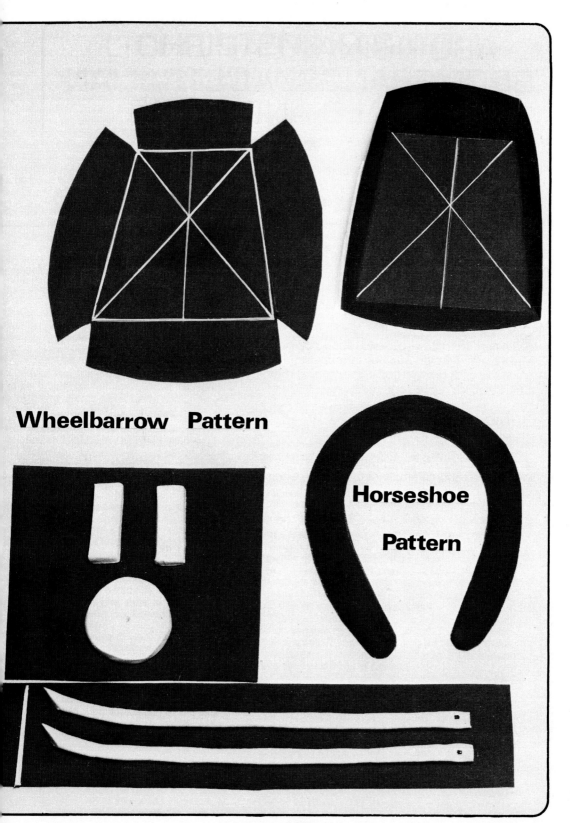

Wheelbarrow Pattern

Horseshoe Pattern

ABORIGINAL CARVINGS, BOOMERANGS, AUSTRALIAN ANIMALS AND BIRDS

Boomerang and wildflower arrangement: See page 92

Motifs such as these are suitable for a boy's cake.

1. Use brown food coloring in the cake covering. Leave to set.

2. Cut out patterns.

3. Place pattern in position, and outline motifs around the sides of the cake with a darning needle.

4. Outline motifs with a No. 00 tube and royal icing. Note – motifs may be piped freehand onto cake if you wish.

5. When dry, tip with brown food coloring.
Motifs may be also cut out in modelling paste, rolled out very finely, painted when dry with brown food coloring, and then attached to cake with royal icing. See welcome home ornament page 48

To make boomerang:
1. Cut pattern.

2. Using dowel, roll out modelling paste as finely as practicable, place pattern in position, and carefully cut out with scalpel. Smooth around the edge with fingers.

3. Mark with scalpel. Leave flat until thoroughly dried.

4. Paint with brown food coloring. A second coat may be necessary.

SMALL BLUE SHELL

A small blue shell moulded from a bought plastic shell and filled with apple blossom, forget-me-nots and fern makes a dainty ornament suitable for a small birthday cake. Place a tiny iced doll in the centre for a christening cake or a ring in the centre for an engagement cake, and surround with flowers. Other flower suggestions – Cecil Brunner roses, hyacinths, snowdrops, bouvardia, lily-of-the-valley, Michaelmas daisies and karume azaleas.

Method:
1. Separate the two halves as shown.

2. Roll out modelling paste in pale blue as finely as practicable, place in shell which has been cornfloured so it won't stick, and press firmly all over with fingers to ensure transfer of pattern to paste.

3. Tip on to board, and with scalpel cut carefully around marked edge. Replace and leave to set. Make other half in the same way.

To assemble:
1. Take sufficient modelling paste (the same color as shell) to fill the base to give a slightly rounded appearance. Lightly moisten base with water so it will stick, place cushion of paste into base and with fingers, taper to edge.

2. Place a piece of wired tulle and loops of pale blue ribbon (half width) into base and immediately arrange flowers. To wire tulle and ribbon, see posy of spring flowers page 23
Finally position lid firmly into soft paste, securing if necessary with royal icing.
Flowers required: 11 apple blossom
                           10 moulded forget-me-nots
                            3 maidenhair fern

DEBUTANTE'S POSY

Decorated cake: See page 168

This lovely posy is not only suitable for a debutante's cake, but would look just as attractive on a 21st birthday or anniversary cake. Posy may be removed from cake and kept as a memento.

Flowers required: 13 small roses in shades of pink
                   4 sprays each of blue hyacinths and forget-me-nots
                   6 sprays pink bouvardia
                   5 leaves

Have flowers made and ready to arrange immediately into base.

To make posy:
1. Cut a strip of tulle about 4 cm (1½ inches) and one and a half times the measurement of circumference of base. Fold until desired size of scallop is obtained, carefully pin all thicknesses together and cut scallops. Using a needle and cotton, run a gathering thread along straight edge and leave for the time being.

2. Color modelling paste pastel pink, the main color of the flower spray. Roll out modelling paste with dowel so that centre is about 1 cm (⅜ inch) thick tapering to the edge, and cut a circle 10 cm (4 inches).

3. Draw up gathering thread, fit around edge of base and set in position with a little royal icing. You might find it necessary to place a pin here and there around the edge to hold in position while you do it.

4. Take two lengths of ribbon each about 61 cm (24 inches), one pink and one blue. Loop as shown, securing beneath loops with a short twist of wire, allowing tails to fall from the base and place in position.

5. Place roses in position securing with a little royal icing, raising the four centre roses slightly if necessary with a little modelling paste. Add flower sprays and place leaves in position with royal icing. Leave flat to dry thoroughly. Posy may be raised from cake by placing two small roses at back near top edge and securing with a run of royal icing around the lower edge of posy where it touches the cake.

Note – base may also be made from plastic fondant (the cake covering). It will take longer to set but will give you more time to assemble the posy.

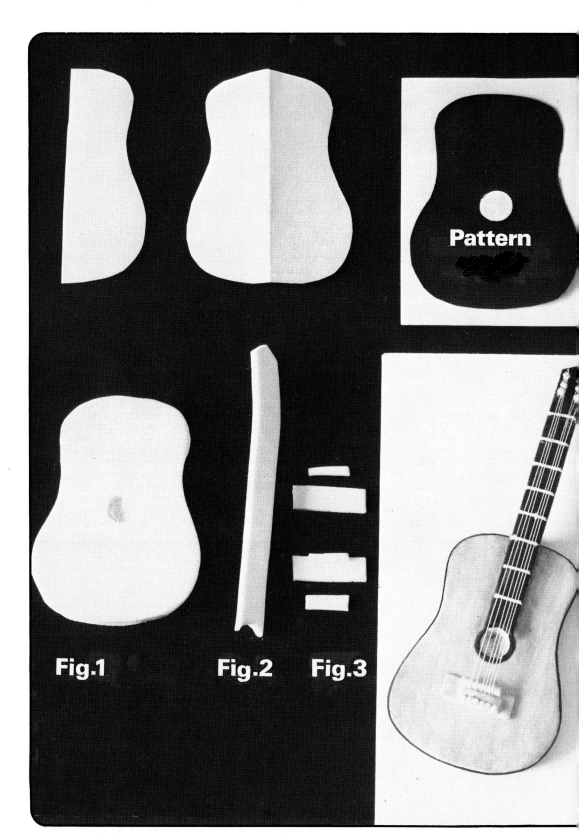

Pattern

Fig.1   **Fig.2**   **Fig.3**

GUITAR

A guitar is very popular with young people and is suitable for a boy's birthday cake. You will find it easy to make if you follow the step by step instructions.

Measurements:
Overall length of guitar 15 cm (5⅞ inches)
Fig. 1 Length 8.2 cm (3¼ inches)
Width across widest part at top 4½ cm (1¾ inches)
Width across widest part at bottom 6 cm (2⅜ inches)
Width across centre 4 cm (1⅝ inches)
Thickness about 4 mm (³/₁₆ inch)
Fig. 2 Length 10½ cm (4⅛ inch)
Width 1 cm (⅜ inch)
Fig. 3 Strip 2½ cm x 9 mm (1 x ⅜ inch) rolled out finely

To make guitar:
1. Cut a pattern for Fig. 1 and Fig. 2 (optional). To cut an accurate pattern, see Hints for the Decorator No. 16.

2. Roll out modelling paste with dowel thickness required, place pattern in position, and cut out Fig. 1 with scalpel. Top must be smooth and free of any cracks, otherwise it will show when painted. With finger, round off top edge. Using a scalpel, cut a small hole where shown about 4 mm (³/₁₆ inch) in diameter and about 3 mm (⅛ inch) deep. Insert top of pencil to neaten. Leave flat to set.

3. Roll out modelling paste as finely as practicable, and cut a strip with long-bladed knife, the measurements for Fig. 2. Shape top with scalpel as shown, and bottom curved to fit hole. Leave flat on modelling board to set, resting top end over edge of board to shape.

4. Roll out modelling paste very finely, and cut a strip Fig. 3 measurements. Roll a small piece of paste between fingers, and cut a small strip for bridge (to rest strings) about 1½ cm (⁹/₁₆ inch), and attach to Fig. 3 with a touch of water as shown. Leave for a few minutes, moisten back with water, and position on to Fig. 1. Leave for one day to completely set before proceeding.

5. Paint back and sides of Fig. 1 and Fig. 2 brown, leaving back of Fig. 2 unpainted where it is attached to Fig. 1. Paint top of Fig. 1 a golden color (yellow with a little brown).

6. When dry, attach Fig. 2 to Fig. 1 with royal icing a shown and leave to set.

To complete:
1. Use cotton for the strings – cut six, longer than required. With a No. 1 tube, squeeze a run of royal icing along base of Fig. 3 and attach the six strings, easing into position with a needle. Place a finely rolled strip (paint the same color as top of guitar when dry) over ends to secure as shown in Fig. 3. Leave to thoroughly set, otherwise when securing the other end they will pull out. Pipe six accentuated dots where shown. When dry, tip silver.

2. Hold the end of each of the six strings in turn firmly with tweezers and attach to top (three on either side) with a dot of royal icing. Leave to set and carefully cut surplus cotton away with scissors. If necessary, squeeze another dot of royal icing on top to neaten. Tip silver.

3. Pipe three accentuated dots of royal icing on either side at top to represent screws, leave white.

BOOK FOR BOY'S 21st

Decorated cake: See page 168

Decorated cake shows an arrangement of daisies and fern. Wildflowers would also be suitable. Choose from flannel flowers, Christmas bush, Christmas bells, brown boronia, wattle and gumnuts.
Mould in color of own choice – centre a contrasting color to cover.
Measurements: Cover 12½ x 9 cm (4½ x 3½ inches) rolled out as finely as practicable
Centre 10 x 8 cm (4 x 3 inches) about 1 cm (³⁄₈ inch thick)

Method:
Cover Using dowel, roll out paste, place pattern in position and cut out with long bladed knife. Using tip of souvenir spoon, press around edge to give an attractive finish. Leave to set.
Centre Using dowel, roll out paste, place pattern in position and cut out with long-bladed knife. Taper corners with forefinger and mark down the centre with a ruler. Moisten back and position immediately on to cover. If cover has not set, leave centre to dry, then attach with a little royal icing.

To complete:
Pipe key with a No. 3 tube and greeting with a No. OO tube. If you wish the date of birthday could also be piped. When dry, tip in either silver or gold, also sides of book.
Place ribbon down the centre and add a knot ribbon bow, securing with a little royal icing.

Book Pattern

CANDLES

Moulded candles are easy to make and could be used in a Christmas decoration – see Christmas roses, holly and candles page 70 An addition of a tall slim candle makes an attractive ornament for a wedding cake see page 164

To make moulded candle (a):
Wick. Roll a tiny piece of paste between fingers to shape wick as shown. Leave to dry.

Candle:
1. Roll an amount of modelling paste onto the palm of your hand into a smooth ball.

2. Roll back and forth beneath finger tips (on a table cloth so it won't slip), and cut length and thickness required. Short candles as in a Christmas decoration can stand upright to dry. Make a hole in the top with a needle to take wick.

3. Paint candle sides red, leaving top diameter white, and allow to dry thoroughly.

4. Pipe a little softened royal icing from top of candle and allow it to trickle down the sides. It is possible some red from the candle will be absorbed into the royal icing and discolor it. Leave to dry, then repaint wax carefully with white water paint.

5. On completion of candle, insert wick into top and secure with royal icing. Tip top of wick brown.

To make tall slim candle (b)
Leave candle white as in decoration, or mould in color. Make in the same manner as for (a). When rolling back and forth beneath fingers, apply a little more pressure as you work towards the top of candle, to graduate it. Candle measures 13 cm (5 inches). Cut length required, and with tips of fingers, draw out a tiny piece of paste from the centre to form a wick. By this time, paste should be firm. Lie down to set.

Small candles: (c)
Candles are sometimes called for on a birthday cake. In that case, use small bought candles. Graduated candles can look attractive arranged either on two sides on the board or along the top edge of two sides of a cake. Candles may also be arranged at the back around the curve of a round cake or in a horseshoe shape on the top of a cake.

To graduate candles:
Lie candles graduated on your modelling board, and mark with long-bladed knife as shown.
Using scissors, cut each candle where marked, and with a No. 20 small petal tube, pipe a rose around the base.
Stand on waxed paper to dry and attach to cake with royal icing. Position the tallest candle first, then arrange candles graduating from either side.

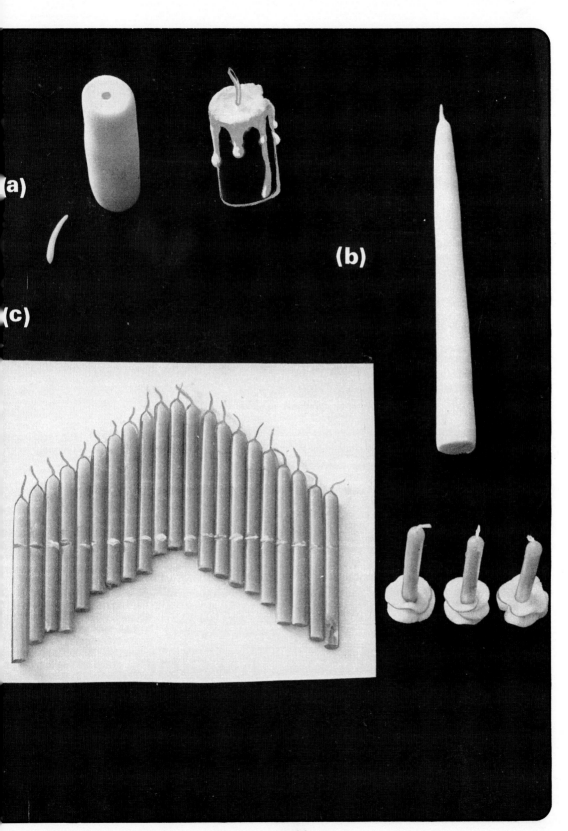

(a)

(b)

(c)

4

Cakes for all Occasions

This chapter gives you a wonderful variety of decorated cakes which I know you will appreciate because of their simplicity and dainty appearance.

To help you, I have given a general description of each cake and the estimated number of flowers required to make the floral arrangements. This, of course, is a guideline only, as no two decorators will make and arrange flowers in exactly the same way.

CARNATION WEDDING CAKE

This three-tier wedding cake, simple in design, has been decorated with pale pink carnations combined with small white flowers. You will notice the centre has been arranged in a diamond effect, the reason being the cake was out of balance (the centre cake was too big for the bottom tier) and it was requested the cake be not cut. If you are decorating a lot of cakes, you will often find that a cake will be too deep or too big and you are requested not to cut, so you are left with only one course, to ice and decorate as it is. To overcome that, turn the middle tier at an angle, and on completion, it will not be noticeable.

Flowers have been arranged on opposite corners, which gives a clear view of each tier.

Flowers required:

Bottom tier	2 carnations
	7 sprays small white flowers
Middle tier	2 carnations (slightly smaller)
	5 sprays small white flowers
Top tier	3 carnations
	12 sprays small white flowers

Doll Birthday Cake. Instructions, see page 162. Pattern page 84

Welcome to Deborah Susan. Instructions page 162

Identical Cakes. Instructions page 156

147

ROSES AND HYACINTHS

Lovely pale lemon roses and white hyacinths make an eye-catching arrangement on this two-tier round wedding cake. A cake such as this would require a flawless covering, as the only pipe work is simple straight extension edged in lace around the base of the cake with small dots piped directly above.

Flowers required:

Bottom tier each spray   2 full blown roses
                                      8 sprays hyacinths
                                      4 leaves
Top tier   2 full blown roses (wired)
                                      9 sprays hyacinths
                                      3 leaves

DOLL BIRTHDAY CAKE

A cake to delight any small girl on her birthday. A round butter cake, covered with swirls of marshmallow, has been decorated on top with a doll and pink piped roses. Tiny dolls in varying colors (one for each small guest) and candles have been placed around the base of the cake.

To decorate dolls, see page 80 . Photograph page 146

DAISIES AND HYACINTHS

Daisies and hyacinths, a combination suitable for a spring wedding, have been arranged in dainty sprays on this eye-catching two-tier cake.

Straight extension has been edged in lace – note how the lace has been positioned at the corners. Narrow ribbon and piped dots form a band around each cake above the extension. Sprays of embroidery have been piped on opposite corners of cake and the addition of tiny birds tipped in silver complete the design.

Flowers required:

Bottom tier – each spray 9 daisies
                                   10 hyacinths

Top tier   18 daisies
                                   18 hyacinths

HAPPY BIRTHDAY CORAL

A pretty embroidered band of forget-me-not sprays outlined in lace softly frames the lovely floral arrangement of pale pink roses, mauve hyacinths, pink bouvardia and white bouvardia on this attractive birthday cake. Rounded extension edged in lace has been finished on the lower edge in a single scallop piped with a No. 00 tube and forms the base design.

Flowers required: 8 roses graduating to buds
about 4 doz hyacinths and bouvardia
5 leaves

NOEL

Christmas roses, holly leaves and berries with looped red ribbon and two small white candles make the attractive and simple decoration on this Noel cake. Berry and leaf design piped with a No. 00 tube and tipped with food coloring when dry, follows the crimper work around the top edge of the cake. Pipe a shell base with either a No. 5 tube or a No. 35 tube and immediately add colored cashews with tweezers. Add a scallop directly above with a No. 3 tube. Finally, pipe greeting, tip when dry and place red ribbon around cake, securing with a bow in front.

Cake is 25 x 15 cm (10 x 6 inches). Use a 20 cm (8 inch) cake and cut off 5 cm (2 inches) from one side of the cake, joining at one end with a little fondant.

Flowers required: 2 roses
5 holly leaves
3 sprigs holly berries

ROSES AND DAISIES

Single roses lightly brushed with yellow around the base and yellow centred white daisies give this two-tiered wedding cake a clean, crisp look.

Tiny scallops with a picot added, outline the lower edge of the off-centred V shaped extension, while small pieces of narrow ribbon about 13 mm (½ inch) long have been inserted above the extension about 19 mm (¾ inch) apart. An embroidered leaf design has been piped between each piece of ribbon and lace added either side to form a band. Two tiny birds added to both tiers complete the design.

Flowers required:

Bottom tier	3 roses	
	8 daisies	
	4 sprays of fern	
Top tier	6 roses	
	9 daisies	
	5 sprays of fern	

155

CECIL BRUNNER ROSES

Lovely sprays of Cecil Brunner roses adorn this elegant three-tier wedding cake. Straight extension banded by narrow ribbon has been finished on the top edge with a tiny scallop. Lace applied to the sides of the cake falls softly over the opposite corners and frames the sprays of roses. Tiny birds complete the design. Cut a pattern for outline of lace, place in position on cake and outline carefully with a darning needle. Position lace pieces with royal icing.

Flowers required:

Bottom tier – each spray	12 Cecil Brunner roses
	about 15 small white flowers
Middle tier – each spray	9 Cecil Brunner roses
	about 12 small white flowers
Top tier	4 medium roses
	4 Cecil Brunner roses
	about 18 small white flowers

IDENTICAL CAKES

Two cream-colored cakes on which sprays of full blown roses and white daisies have been arranged were the choice of this bride. The pipe work on the cake is very simple for a beginner.

A No. 5 tube has been used to pipe a shell around the base of each cake above which interlacing loops have been piped with a No. 00 tube. Accentuated dots piped in a half circle above loops complete the base design.

A forget-me-not and bow design has been piped freehand around the sides of the cakes, and a small ribbon bow attached at each corner with a dot of royal icing.

Flowers required:

each cake 2 full blown roses
4 small daisies
8 hyacinths
3 rosebuds
3 leaves

Photograph page 147

HEARTS AND ORANGE BLOSSOM

Hearts and orange blossom, a lovely idea for a three-tiered wedding cake for the bride-to-be. Rounded extension edged in lace, topped with a pretty embroidery band and finished with a narrow band of ribbon, forms an attractive base for this simple and elegant design. Hearts embroidered and outlined in lace add a distinctive touch.

Orange blossoms and hyacinths, a perfect combination for this design, have been arranged on opposite corners, while the top tier features a raised posy.

Flowers required:

Bottom tier – each spray	12 orange blossom
	7 sprays hyacinths
Middle tier – each spray	10 orange blossom
	7 sprays hyacinths
Top tier	16 orange blossom
	20 sprays hyacinths

OVAL TWO-TIER 21st

Cecil Brunner roses and a combination of tiny flowers such as bouvardia, hyacinths, forget-me-nots, lilac and eriostemon form the sprays on this elaborate pale pink 21st birthday cake.

The design itself is quite simple with V shaped extension finished on top and lower edge with a tiny scallop. The flowers make the cake elaborate, and it will be time-consuming to make the number required for the cake, but your efforts will be well rewarded with praise and congratulations.

Flowers required:

Bottom tier	12 to 14 Cecil Brunner roses
	About 14 doz. small flowers – a combination of pink bouvardia and white bouvardia, blue hyacinths, eriostemon, lilac and forget-me-nots
	About 12 tiny leaves
Top tier	10 to 12 Cecil Brunner roses
	About 6 doz. tiny flowers as for bottom tier
	About 6 tiny leaves

Photograph page 167

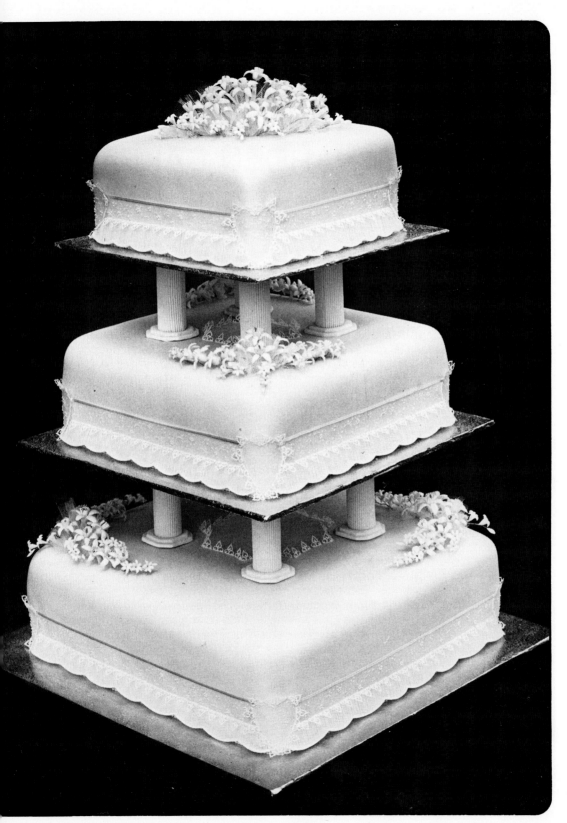

DOLLY VARDEN CAKE

A cake such as this would be suitable for a girl eight to 12 years of age. Cake was baked in a dolly varden tin or you could use a pudding bowl.

Buy a small doll about 15.2 cm (6 inches) tall from a chain stores and cut off just below the waist. Roll out modelling paste and cut a small bodice to fit and attach to doll with a little water. Cover cake with fondant and when set, cut out just sufficient fondant and a little cake if necessary, insert doll to ensure a nice firm fit. Cut out peplum from modelling paste – two layers, one smaller – and position around doll, securing at top edge with a little royal icing. When set, embroider with cornelli work.

Starting at the base of the cake, pipe rows of frills using a leaf tube, each row slightly overlapping the previous row. Pipe sprays of embroidery with a No. OO tube. Gather a small length of tulle with needle and cotton for hat, secure to head with royal icing and several piped roses and leaves in the centre. A frill of tulle has been added around the skirt and secured with a little royal icing and piped roses and leaves.

SWAN CHRISTENING CAKE

This lovely round christening cake features a spray of karume azaleas, forget-me-nots, and tiny swans. Background has been painted directly on to cake using a fine paint brush and food coloring when covering has completely set. Pretty embroidered tulle overskirt has been secured with forget-me-nots. Narrow pink ribbon around cake completes the design.

Flowers required: 6 karume azaleas
9 moulded forget-me-nots
4 sets of leaves
About 18 forget-me-nots around side of cake

Tulle overskirt. Cut tulle about 5 cm (about 2 inches) deep and one and a half times the circumference of the cake in length. Fold to the required number of scallops, pin and cut through all thicknesses. Cut a second layer in the same manner about 4 cm (1½ inches) deep. Gather the two layers of tulle at top edge together with needle and thread, draw to fit cake and secure with wired forget-me-nots. Embroider with a No. OO tube.

To mould swans, see page 114

BRIDAL SPRAYS

This dainty three-tier wedding cake features bridal sprays and a small china shoe filled with rosebuds, lily-of-the-valley, hyacinths and bouvardia.
Pretty extension edged in lace and freehand embroidery form the base design. Four small hearts, latticed and outlined in lace, make an unusual centrepiece beneath the pillars.
Flowers required:
Bottom and middle tiers   4 rosebuds and about
                         12 sprays of small flowers
Top tier   9 rosebuds and about
                         18 sprays of small flowers

WELCOME TO DEBORAH SUSAN

A dainty spray of karume azaleas, snowdrops and forget-me-nots frame the beautiful card depicting two tiny angels on this lovely pale pink christening cake. Straight extension edged in lace and banded by narrow pink ribbon (cut in half) forms an attractive base. Pretty sprays of forget-me-nots have been embroidered around the top edge of the cake.
Flowers required: 7 karume azaleas
                    15 snowdrops
                     3 sprays forget-me-nots
                     3 fishbone fern

To make card:
Roll out paste smoothly, cut out card with a long-bladed knife, and then cut edge of card into scallops with scalpel. Add narrow pink ribbon, securing at the back with royal icing so the edging shows. Pictures of angels were obtained from christening wrapping paper, traced, cut out in modelling paste, painted and attached to card with royal icing. Forget-me-nots are piped directly on to card and add a touch of glitter with tweezers to form the centre of each flower. Pipe embroidery with a No. OO tube, and tip silver when dry.

Photograph page 147

COMBINATION 21st BIRTHDAY AND ENGAGEMENT CAKE

This two-tiered cake is a lovely idea for a combination 21st birthday and engagement cake. The off-centred V-shaped extension has been edged in lace and accentuated dots piped directly above. Forget-me-nots and true lovers' bows form dainty sprays on the sides and opposite corners of the cakes.

Pale pink roses have been piped around the base of 21 graduated candles arranged on opposite corners of the board. A key piped with a No. 3 tube, tipped in silver, has been placed beneath the pillars with two bluebirds. Sprays of pink roses, blue hyacinths and forget-me-nots are arranged on opposite corners of bottom tier.

The top tier reserved for the engagement has been set at an angle, and the spray arranged trailing to the front of the cake. Two bluebirds and the young couple's names written with No. OO tube tipped in silver complete the design.

Flowers required:

Bottom tier each spray   3 roses
                             2 sprays each of hyacinths forget-me-nots and bouvardia
                             3 leaves
Top tier   5 roses
                             6 sprays each of hyacinths and bouvardia
                             2 sprays forget-me-nots
                             5 leaves

Swan Christening Cake. Instructions page 160

166

Pale Mauve Wedding Cake. Instructions page 172

Oval two-tier 21st Birthday Cake. Instructions page 158

167

168

CONGRATULATIONS PAUL

Here is a very simply styled cake suitable for a boy's 21st birthday. Use a No. 35 small tube for the base. Cut off the flow of icing cleanly as you pipe, leaving sufficient space to pipe a dot with a No. 2 or No. 3 tube in between each shell. Next add scalloped edge above also in a No. 2 tube.

Add a narrow band of ribbon around cake, securing each corner with a knot ribbon bow. Pipe scallops on either side of ribbon, using a No. 0 tube to match scallops around the base of cake.

A Florentine design has been used around the top edge of the cake – a suitable design for a masculine cake. Using a No. 0 tube, first outline a continuous curve running through the centre of the design. Then add small and large scrolls on either side of curve. Finally, add a small piped leaf, which is just a dot of royal icing drawn to a point.

Piped daisies have been used here, but of course, moulded daisies may be substituted.

Flowers required: About 12 piped daisies or
                   9 moulded daisies
                   Several sprays of maidenhair fern

To make book see page 138

DEBUTANTE'S CAKE

The simple styling of this lovely cake would please any debutante. It would also be suitable for a birthday cake. The posy has been mounted on to a base so it may be removed and kept.

The built-out extension is piped with a No. 3 tube in pink, which forms a very attractive base when the soft pink shows through the fine white extension lines. The top edge is finished with lace, the lower edge with a single row with a No. 00 tube.

A dainty band of embroidery falls softly over the edge of the cake, the lower edge outlined in lace, the inner edge in tiny scallops which form a circle on top of the cake and frames the beautiful lift-off posy of pale pink roses, bouvardia, blue hyacinths and forget-me-not sprays.

To make posy see page 134

BUTTERCUPS AND DAISIES

A delightful way to say happy Easter – a basket containing an Easter egg surrounded by buttercups and daisies. This prize-winning egg was made from sugar, but you could instead use a chocolate egg. Bunnies were cut out in modelling paste, lightly moistened on back with water and immediately positioned on egg, and when dry, painted with food coloring. Scattered around bunnies are moulded forget-me-nots and sprigs of grass.

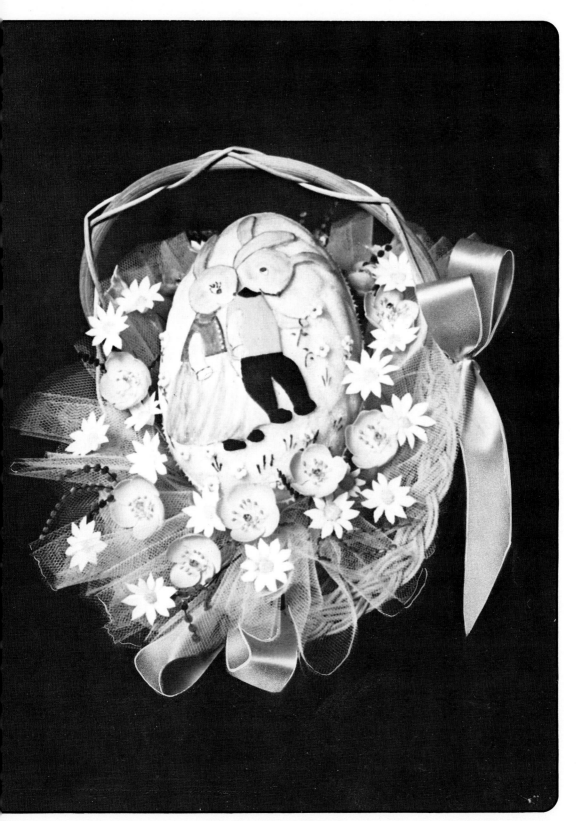

TWO-TIER ROUND WEDDING CAKE

This two-tier wedding cake has been simply styled with straight extension edged in lace forming the base design. A narrow band of ribbon has been placed around the cake and finished with a pretty bow in front. Pipe scallop and dropped loops beneath ribbon with a No. 0 tube and add accentuated dots.

Flowers required:

Bottom tier – each spray	4 graduated roses
	6 sprays small flowers
	3 rose leaves
Top tier	5 roses
	15 sprays small flowers
	3 rose leaves

PALE MAUVE WEDDING CAKE

This unusual arrangement of three 20 x 20 cm (8 x 8 inch) pale mauve cakes with sprays of lovely yellow full blown roses and mauve hyacinths might appeal to a bride who is looking for something really outstanding.

The roses have been wired, which elevates the arrangements, improves greatly the appearance of the cake and makes it so much easier to add the small flowers. Notice how the board has been cut to allow the two base cakes to fit together.

Extension edged in lace forms an attractive base around cakes. Sprays of embroidery have been piped freehand with a No. 00 tube and cakes finished around top edge with a narrow band of pale mauve ribbon, secured in front with a small bow. Tiny birds complete the design.

Flowers required:

2 base cakes each cake	2 full blown roses
	10 to 12 sprays mauve hyacinths
	3 leaves
Top cake	2 full blown roses
	8 sprays mauve hyacinths
	3 leaves

Photograph page 167

ROSES AND FUCHSIAS

Open roses, fuchsias and snowdrops have been arranged in attractive sprays on this three-tier heart shaped cake. A No. 35 small shell tube has been used around the base of each cake. A scallop has been piped directly above with a No. 3 tube from which interlacing loops have been piped with a No. 00 tube. Pretty freehand embroidery has been piped the depth of the cakes.

Flowers required:

Bottom tier	6 open roses with a touch of pink
	4 pink and mauve fuchsias
	about 18 snowdrops
Middle tier	5 open roses
	4 fuchsias
	about 18 snowdrops
Top tier	2 open roses
	6 fuchsias
	about 15 snowdrops

A SHOWER FOR GLENYS

A pale blue cup and saucer tipped in gold and filled with pink and blue daisies and sprays of white primula – a lovely and novel idea for a shower tea.
This could be a fruit cake, or as this one was, a butter cake with a fondant covering only. Base has been piped in scallops with a No. 5 tube and cake finished with a band of pale blue ribbon.

Flowers required: 18 pink and blue small daisies
             5 sprays primula
             4 fern
             2 daisies and 2 primula and fern trailing across saucer.

Instructions for making cup and saucer — see page 27.

SHOWER FOR JAN

An umbrella filled with dainty flowers makes an attractive ornament for a shower tea cake, but need not be a fruit cake. A butter cake has been baked in a 20 cm (8 inch) round cake tin and covered with orange vienna icing (see recipe). Cover a 25 cm (10 inch) round board with silver paper, place cake in position, spread with icing and lightly swirl with a knife, leaving sufficient cream to pipe a shell border around base. When icing has set, tie a narrow ribbon around side of cake, finishing with a pretty bow in front.

Instructions for making shower umbrella — see Shower Umbrella page 24.
Place umbrella in position, and wire flowers directly into cake.

Flowers required: 11 piped cream roses or moulded rosebuds
             5 sprays blue hyacinths
             4 sprays cream bouvardia
             3 sprays snowdrops
             5 maidenhair fern

DAINTY BESS ROSES

Sprays of pale pink roses, hyacinths and scattered forget-me-nots make the attractive floral arrangements on this three-tier wedding cake. Two-tier cake is also given.
Straight extension edged in lace and finished on the lower edge with accentuated dots forms the base border. Simple embroidery has been piped freehand and cakes finished around the top edge with a narrow band of ribbon.
Flowers required:

Bottom tier	5 roses
each spray	3 rosebuds
	about 14 hyacinths and forget-me-nots
Middle tier	3 roses 2 rosebuds
each spray	about 12 hyacinths and forget-me-nots
Top tier	4 roses
	4 rosebuds
	about 18 hyacinths and forget-me-nots

A CONFIRMATION CAKE

Dainty sprays of Cecil Brunner roses have been arranged around each pillar on the bottom tier and confirmation plaque is supported by an arrangement of flowers wired directly into the cake on the top tier.
Shell border has been piped with a No. 3 tube, also scallop directly above. Cornelli (piped in a No. 00 tube) and crimper work form a band around the base of the cakes and finish with a tiny ribbon bow at each point. A tiny moulded chalice tipped in silver has been positioned in front of cakes with grape and sheaves of wheat piped with a No. 00 tube.

Flowers required:
Bottom tier – each spray 3 Cecil Brunner roses
                          10 small white flowers
Top tier   about 9 Cecil Brunner roses
                          about 18 small white flowers

Ornament, Pattern, and Instructions, see page 119

5
Icing Recipes

MODELLING PASTE

This is the modelling paste I use and recommend. It is essential that it is made carefully and all ingredients measured accurately, otherwise you will not achieve the correct consistency, which is most important when making ornaments – refer Hints for the Decorator No. 6.

Gelatine must be thoroughly dissolved, otherwise the undissolved grains will become like jelly and show up through the paste, making it useless. I stress the point, because so many beginners make that error. If insufficient gelatine is added, paste will not have correct elasticity, while too much gelatine will make the paste like a rubber ball. Experience is the best teacher, and you will know by the feel of the paste when it is right. Do not overdo the glucose – remember it becomes liquid when dissolved.

Some moulded ornaments require a lot of modelling paste, so if making several ornaments, make 450 g (1 lb) of modelling paste, otherwise make up only half the mixture, but be sure you halve all the ingredients.

Ingredients	Metric	Imperial
Pure sifted icing sugar	450 g	1 lb
Gelatine	4 scant teaspoons	4 scant teaspoons
Glucose	2 rounded teaspoons	2 rounded teaspoons
Water	¼ cup	2 fl oz

Method:

1. Sift pure icing sugar into a bowl.

2. Place gelatine and water into a small bowl, stand it in a saucepan containing a little water and dissolve over gentle heat. With that method you will not lose any liquid.

3. When dissolved, add glucose. The liquid should be quite clear before adding to icing sugar.

4. Make a well in the centre of icing sugar and stir in liquid with a knife.

5. Place mixture in a plastic bag and then in a container with a lid, and store at room temperature. Leave to stand about three hours before using.

ROYAL ICING

Royal icing is used for all pipe work and is better beaten by hand as it produces a much better piping consistency. Electrically beaten royal icing gives a false impression of consistency, and on standing, will subside because of aeration in the mixture. Use royal icing freshly beaten to achieve the best results.

Ingredients	Metric	Imperial
1 egg white		
Pure sieved icing sugar	2¼ cups	12 oz
(amount used will depend on		
size of egg white)		
Acetic acid	2 drops	2 drops

Method:
It is a good idea to have a small glass or china bowl and a small wooden spoon set aside exclusively for mixing your royal icing. Place egg white into bowl and gradually add a tablespoon of pure icing sugar at a time, beating well after each addition. Do not be tempted to add too much icing sugar too quickly, you will not achieve the same results. Continue in that manner, add acetic acid as the mixture thickens and continue beating, adding less icing sugar until mixture is thick and firm enough to hold a peak. A soft consistency is required for fine pipe work and firm for shell borders. Place in a container with a lid. Do not leave royal icing uncovered as the air will soon cause a crust on top. It is not necessary to use a whole egg white, a half or even one third will make sufficient royal icing to decorate a cake.

MARSHMALLOW

Ingredients
1 cup water
1 cup sugar
1 tablespoon gelatine
Flavoring and coloring of own choice.

Method:
1. Place first three ingredients into a saucepan.

2. Stir to dissolve sugar.

3. Bring to boil and boil for two minutes.

4. Allow to cool. When slightly thickened, add flavoring and coloring and beat until thick and fluffy. Using a knife, swirl over cake.

PLASTIC FONDANT

An excellent fondant for covering cakes. It is particularly recommended for wedding cakes, ensuring a dazzling white smooth surface, while remaining soft to eat. This recipe is sufficient to cover an average size three-tier wedding cake or a large two-tier cake. Make at least one day before use.

Ingredients	Metric	Imperial
Group 1		
Gelatine	2 tablespoons	1 oz
Water	⅔ cup	5 fl oz
Group 2		
Crystal sugar	2 cups	1 lb
Liquid glucose	⅓ cup	4 oz
Glycerine	6 scant teaspoons	1 oz
Water	⅔ cup	5 fl oz
Cream of tartar	1 level teaspoon	1 level teaspoon
Group 3		
Copha	125 g	4 oz
Pure icing sugar	9 cups	3 lb

Place group 1 in a bowl. To dissolve I prefer to stand bowl in a saucepan containing a little water and dissolve over gentle heat. While it is dissolving – Place group 2 in a saucepan which has been greased lightly around the top with a little copha. Place in sugar thermometer and stir over medium heat until sugar has dissolved and mixture starts to boil. Remove spoon and boil on fast heat until thermometer registers 115 deg. C (240 deg. F).

Remove from heat, allow to cool about five minutes and then stir in dissolved gelatine and flaked copha (group 3). Pour mixture into a large bowl, preferably one with a lid, and stir in icing sugar (group 3) a cupful at a time. Clean down sides of bowl with a spatula, replace lid and leave for 24 hours before use. When required, knead in extra icing sugar to obtain the required consistency.

NET STIFFENER

Use cotton net with net stiffener only when you are making something you want to hold a shape, such as net bootees. Tulle is not suitable.

Recipe – for a small quantity.
> ¼ cup pure icing sugar
> ¼ cup water

Place above in a small saucepan and stir over gentle heat to dissolve. Bring to boil and simmer about three minutes. Cool and store in screw-top jar.
To stiffen net, using tweezers immerse pieces in stiffener, remove, gently pat out any surplus on a towel and place over shape to set.

ALMOND PASTE

An undercoat of almond paste gives a good base for the covering of a cake, and the recipe is sufficient to cover a 20 x 20 cm (8 x 8 inch) cake. First brush over the cake with egg white before covering with almond paste.

Ingredients	Metric	Imperial
Pure icing sugar	3 cups	1 lb
Ground almonds or marzipan meal	1¼ cups	4 oz
Egg yolks, 2		
Sweet sherry	2 tablespoons	2 tablespoons
Sufficient lemon juice to		
mix to a firm dough		

Method:
1. Place sieved pure icing sugar and ground almonds into a bowl. Mix well.

2. Beat egg yolks, add sherry and lemon juice and add to mixture in bowl. Knead to a firm dough, adding a little more icing sugar if too soft and a little more sherry if too firm.

3. Roll out on board lightly dusted with icing sugar, and with aid of rolling pin, place over cake which has been brushed with egg white. Roll over top and down sides with rolling pin, and rub with palms of hands lightly dusted with icing sugar to give a nice smooth surface. If using marzipan, leave one day before covering, if using almonds, leave two or three days, to prevent almond oil from seeping through and staining cover.

BASIC BUTTER CAKE

Ingredients	Metric	Imperial
Butter or margarine (softened)	125 g (½ cup)	4 oz
Castor sugar	¾ cup	6 oz
Self-raising flour	2 cups	8 oz
Eggs – large	2	2
Vanilla essence	1 teaspoon	1 teaspoon
Milk	½ cup	½ cup

Place all ingredients in a large bowl, beat with electric mixer on high speed for three minutes.
Bake in a 20 cm (8 inch) round cake tin in a moderate oven, 180 deg. C to 190 deg. C (350 deg. F to 375 deg. F), for about 45 minutes.
Note. Lemon or orange cake – Add the finely grated rind of 1 lemon or 1 orange and 2 teaspoons of lemon juice or orange juice.

PLASTIC ICING

This is a very good plastic icing recipe used widely by cake decorators, with assured success. It gives a lovely smooth covering and remains soft to eat. This recipe is sufficient to cover a 20 x 20 cm (8 x 8 inch) cake or a 250 g (½ lb) fruit cake mixture.

Ingredients	Metric	Imperial
Pure sieved icing sugar	6 cups	2 lb
Liquid glucose	½ cup	½ cup
Glycerine	1 tablespoon	1 tablespoon
Gelatine	5 teaspoons	½ oz
Water	¼ cup	¼ cup
Flavoring of own choice	several drops sufficient to flavor	

Method:

1. Sieve icing sugar into a bowl.

2. Place gelatine and water into a small bowl, stand in a saucepan containing a little water (to a depth of about 4 cm – 1 ½ inches) and dissolve over gentle heat until gelatine has been thoroughly dissolved. Using that method, you will not boil the mixture, nor will you lose any liquid in dissolving. Remove from heat.

3. Stir in glucose and glycerine (with bowl still standing in hot water) until dissolved. Replace over gentle heat if necessary to completely dissolve.

4. Stir liquid into sieved icing sugar.

5. Remove from bowl and knead well until icing becomes smooth and pliable. Add coloring and flavoring and it is ready for use. Add a little extra icing sugar should the mixture be too soft. Icing may be stored in an airtight container at room temperature until required. **Note** – if you do not wish to cover the cake after making icing, don't knead in all the icing sugar. Reserve say about a cupful and knead it in when ready to apply to cake.

VIENNA ICING

Ingredients	Metric	Imperial
Butter	½ cup	4 oz
Icing sugar	1½ cups	8 oz
Orange juice (or milk)	2 tablespoons	2 tablespoons

1. Cream butter well.

2. Gradually beat in sifted icing sugar alternately with fruit juice until thick and creamy.

3. Spread over cake with knife.

HINTS FOR MAKING SUCCESSFUL FRUIT CAKES

Rounding off metric measurements, you should use a reliable, well-proportioned recipe, eg 250 g (½ lb) each of butter and brown sugar, 1 250 g (2½ lb) fruit and 315 g (10 oz) plain flour or 60 g (2 oz) self-raising flour to 250 g (8 oz) plain flour in a 250 g (½ lb) cake as the basic ingredients.

Fruit cakes are referred to as 250 g (½ lb) and 500 g (1 lb) mixtures according to the quantity of butter and sugar used, **not** as the **total** weight of the cake when baked.
Bake a 125 g (¼ lb) mixture in a 15 x 15 cm (6 x 6 inch) tin.
Bake a 250 g (½ lb) mixture in a 20 x 20 cm (8 x 8 inch) tin.
Bake a 500 g (1 lb) mixture in a 25 x 25 cm (10 x 10 inch) tin.
Bake a 750 g (1½ lb) mixture in a 30 x 30 cm (12 x 12 inch) tin.

To ensure nice square corners of cake, care should be taken in lining the tin. Don't allow paper to become embedded in the mixture, or when removing, the paper will pull away some of the cake.

Always wash currants, raisins and sultanas and spread evenly on trays to dry, remove pips and stalks and cut up large pieces of fruit such as dates, apricots, raisins, or others. Do not mince fruit, it cannot be separated by the cake mixture.

Do not use damp fruit.

Allow fruit and nuts to stand for several days or even longer in screw topped jar with spirits, as it improves the flavor of the cake.

Have eggs and butter at room temperature, add eggs singly, beating after each addition, but do not overheat as it tends to thin the mixture and separate the creamed ingredients.

Eggs and butter may be beaten in mixer, then placed in large mixing bowl and mixed by hand. If mixture separates after the addition of eggs, take a little flour from the weighed quantity for the cake and blend through the mixture.

Sift spices together with flour and salt twice to ensure even blending.

If the creamed mixture is thin because of overbeating or the heat of the day, place basin in refrigerator to firm mixture before adding the weight of the fruit, and so reduce the possibility of the fruit sinking through the over-soft cake mixture.

After placing mixture in tins, spread evenly, then bump the tins several times on the table to settle the mixture.

Rich fruit cakes need not be cooked the same day as they are mixed. They may be stored in refrigerator for several days, allowed to thaw to reach room termperature, then baked.

Bake in a slow oven for the whole cooking time. Do not put into a moderate or hot oven and then reduce heat. That practice results in the surface of the cake being baked too quickly, and the result is a hard surface and a crack on top.

When cake is removed from oven, sprinkle with two or three tablespoons brandy, sherry or rum, which is immediately absorbed into the cake. Cover with alfoil or greaseproof paper and then in several thicknesses of paper or towel.

Fruit cakes improve with keeping. Cake may be made several months before required.

RICH WEDDING CAKE MIXTURE

General Instructions, see page 189

This recipe I can recommend not only for that all-important cake, the wedding cake, but also for any special occasion cake as well as the Christmas cake. It is a rich moist cake, cuts beautifully and has a delicious flavor.

Recipe for 500 g (1 lb) 25 cm (10 inch) cake.

Ingredients	Metric	Imperial
Sultanas	3 cups	1 lb
Currants	3⅓ cups	1 lb
Raisins	3 cups	1 lb
Glace apricots or pineapple	¾ cup	4 oz
Prunes	1⅓ cups	8 oz
Chopped mixed peel	1½ cups	8 oz
Glace cherries	1½ cups	8 oz
Almonds – chopped	1 cup	4 oz
Walnuts – chopped	1 cup	4 oz
Dates	¾ cup	4 oz
Sherry, rum or brandy	½ cup	½ cup
Butter	2 cups	1 lb
Brown sugar	3 cups	1 lb
Eggs – large	10	10
Golden syrup or honey	1 tablespoon	1 tablespoon
Marmalade, plum or raspberry jam	1 tablespoon	1 tablespoon
Glycerine	1 tablespoon	1 tablespoon
Vanilla essence	1 teaspoon	1 teaspoon
Almond essence	1 teaspoon	1 teaspoon
Grated rind and juice of 1 lemon		
Plain flour	4 cups	1 lb
Self-raising flour	1 cup	4 oz
Mixed spice	2 teaspoons	2 teaspoons
Salt	½ teaspoon	½ teaspoon
bi-carbonate of soda (optional)	¼ teaspoon	¼ teaspoon

Method

1. Wash and dry all fruits. Cut up apricots, prunes, dates, cherries and raisins.

2. Place fruits and nuts in jar and cover. Stand several days if possible or at least overnight in spirit used.

3. Cream butter and sugar well, add eggs one at a time and mix thoroughly.

4. Add essences, glycerine, golden syrup, jam, lemon rind and juice.

5. Add sifted dry ingredients and fruit alternately to mixture until all is added.

6. Line a 25 cm (10 inch) cake tin with two sheets of brown paper, bringing the paper about 4 cm (1½ inches) above the tin.

7. Bake in a slow oven 140 deg. C to 150 deg. C (275 deg. F to 300 deg. F) for about 5 to 5½ hours.

8. When baked trickle 2 or 3 tablespoons of sherry, rum or brandy over cake while still hot, then wrap in several thicknesses of paper and a towel and allow to cool slowly. This slow method cooling seals in the steam and helps keep cake moist.

9. Remove from tin when cold and re-wrap until required.

Index